MIDGES, MAPS & MUESLI

HELEN KRASNER

MIDGES
MAPS
& MUESLI

An Account of a 5,000 Mile Walk
Round the Coast of Britain

GARTH PUBLICATIONS

1998

Published by Garth Publications
15 The Hallsteads,
Kniveton, Ashbourne
Derbyshire, DE6 1JT

Reprinted 2007

ISBN 978-0-9533801-0-7

A catalogue record for this book is available from the British Library

Printed in Great Britain

Contents

Acknowledgements

So many people helped me on this walk that it is impossible to mention them individually without leaving someone out. However, especial thanks are due to Miriam Collard for her general help and back-up, John Lees of Radio Sussex for his encouragement, and my late mother, without whom the whole venture would probably have been impossible.

Chapter 1

Preparations: The Best Laid Plans...

I was lost. I didn't want to believe it, but it was true. The fog had come down suddenly, as often happens on the coast, and it had caught me completely unawares. I could hardly see a yard in front of me, and I had no idea where to go or what to do. I had tried to find my way by compass bearing but it had been no use. For I had lost the footpath when the fog first descended; and with hedges, fences and impenetrable scrub, not to mention a hundred foot drop to the sea somewhere off to my left, I hardly dared move, let alone cut cross-country. Anyway, I reminded myself dismally, I didn't really have much idea how to take a compass bearing. I'd planned to go on a navigation course before starting this walk, but it had been one of the many things I'd meant to do but hadn't—along with training, planning the route, listening to weather forecasts. None of it had actually happened.

I wasn't really afraid, or so I tried to tell myself anyway, and I almost believed it. Actually I felt rather stupid. For while I had expected to get lost at some point on a 5,000 mile walk around the coast of Britain, I had assumed it would be in the Scottish Highlands, on the North Cornish coast, or in some other wild, desolate corner of the country. But no, here I was, on only my tenth day of the walk, a couple of miles from Swanage in Dorset, on a path walked by thousands of tourists every year. I was so close to the town I could hear the traffic in the streets and a cow mooing in a nearly farm. But I might as well have been a thousand miles away for all the good it did me.

As the damp, impenetrable mist swirled around me I took a couple of deep breaths and tried to decide what to do. Well, I thought to myself, trying hard to be rational, I had a tent, a sleeping bag, and enough food. I could survive even if I had to spend the night up there. There was no reason to panic; getting lost wasn't a disaster. Something of the sort had to happen sometime. Anyway, I was a tough, experienced long distance walker, super-fit and entirely confident of my ability to walk right round the coast of Britain safely. Wasn't I?

The answer was no, I wasn't. I was an ordinary woman with time on her hands and a romantic idea, and not much else. And there was no doubt about it now, I was beginning to get scared. It was true that I had enough equipment to spend the night in the hills if necessary, but logic doesn't help much in these situations. It didn't alter the fact that I was cold, lonely, and miserable. I wanted to go home, to sit by the fire and the TV like sane, normal people.

"Why?" I asked myself for the hundredth time in five minutes. Why, why, why had I got myself into this situation? I knew I should have seen the fog coming. Clearly, I thought to myself, I didn't have the knowledge or experience for this sort of walk. I should never have begun it in the first place.

"It's all Miriam's fault," I muttered to myself, quite irrationally, and entirely unfairly. "She started all this. It was her idea."

This wasn't true and I knew it, but it helped a bit to have someone else to blame. Though my old friend Miriam had indeed played a part in it. Had it really been only a few months ago?

It had begun, like many adventures, in a very small way. It was later one evening in early summer, and I was sitting in the front room of Miriam's house in Streatham. We had been friends for over twenty years, and I had recently moved back to Croydon, my home town, after an absence of almost twenty years. I was working as a secretary, temping, and I was quite happy in a vaguely apathetic sort of way. But with no permanent job and no commitments I kept getting the feeling I was missing some kind of opportunity. There were so many things I could do while I had no ties, like write a book, or travel, or …

I was explaining all this to Miriam that evening, though at the time I had no real intention of actually doing any of it. At least, I hadn't until Miriam's enthusiasm took over.

"Well," she said. "You could always walk round the coast of Britain. You've been talking about it for enough years."

It was true; I had thought about walking round Britain before. I can't actually remember when I first got the idea, though during the walk I was to tell various people that I first thought of it when I was a child in the fifties, and an admirer of Dr. Barbara Moore's long distance walking exploits. It was a good story, and I told it so often I finally almost forgot myself whether it was true or false. But anyway, it was an idea I'd had for a long time. It wasn't a burning ambition—nothing that intense—just a vague idea. I'd frequently told friends it "would be a nice thing to do if I ever have the time and the money and no commitments". I didn't see myself as a record-breaking athlete or a great explorer or anything like that. The image I had in mind was more of a kind of female Dick Whittington, a wandering minstrel, as it were. I saw myself meandering slowly through peaceful villages by the sea, chatting to people in pubs, fields and gardens, without a care in the world. The image, of course, never included rain, blisters, unfriendly people, or getting lost in fog. The whole thing was totally unrealistic and I don't think I actually believed I'd ever do it. Until now.

For Miriam is given to fits of infectious enthusiasm, and she now warmed to her subject in a big way.

"Why don't you do it?" she asked. "I mean, what's to stop you? You can stay in youth hostels, or take one of those lightweight tents they do now. I can act as your back-up."

As she continued excitedly, I got caught up in the whole crazy idea, and I suddenly decided, there and then, that I would do it. I really would walk round the whole coast of Britain. Why not? After all, I really didn't have anything better to do.

So, while later on I invented dozens of reasons for the walk for the benefit of reporters and TV interviewers, I was really just trying to give them a good story. For they all seemed quite sure that I must have something important in mind, that I must be trying to break a record, or seeking the meaning of life. But I wasn't. I just wanted to walk round Britain for fun, because it seemed like a nice thing to do.

The coastline of Britain is said to be approximately 6,500 miles long. When I first found this out, soon after deciding to walk round it, I nearly decided to give up there and then; I'd thought it must be a couple of thousand miles at most. I then discovered that when walking round the coast one can actually cover anything from 3,000 to well over 7,000 miles. It all depends on what you mean by "coastline", on which routes you take, whether you walk on roads or paths or beaches, how many rivers you have to skirt around and how many headlands you cut across. But however you do it, I discovered, it's a long trip, realistically taking anything from six to eighteen months. No wonder in the past it had been attempted by relatively few people.

Those who had done it all agreed on one thing—that such trips take a great deal of planning. John Merrill, the first person ever to walk round the coastline of Britain, described spending months buying maps and organising the venture, and the book he wrote included a picture of him surrounded by huge piles of equipment. Vera Andrews, a women who walked round the coast in 1984, spent over a year training and planning her accommodation and routes. I suppose it's not really difficult to see why so much organisation should be necessary. One needs many large-scale maps showing all the minor roads and footpaths, plus clothing and other supplies suitable for months of constant wear and all four seasons; also hiking boots, backpack, and possibly camping equipment. There are routes to be planned and overnight accommodation to be arranged. Then, most people need to organise their affairs back home so that they can be away for an extended period; they may also want to receive mail or have contact addresses for friends and family. The list is endless; it's not surprising that many agree the planning is harder than the actual walking.

I am not, by nature, a planner. I prefer to take things as they come, assuming I can sort out problems as and when they happen. So it never even occurred to me to undertake any systematic organisation of this sort. It just didn't seem necessary, and besides, it sounded like a lot of work. Not at all what I'd had in mind when I conjured up my wandering vagabond image. I felt sure I could arrange things as I went, picking up items I needed en route if necessary. So I simply decided, somewhat arbitrarily, on my departure date—March 1st 1986—and planned to buy a minimal amount of walking and camping equipment plus the first few maps before I went. My long-suffering mother agreed to forward mail to addresses that I would arrange later, and Miriam would act as general "back-up" if needed.

That was all I did. I reckoned the rest of the walk would take care of itself. To some this would appear a foolhardy and potentially disastrous way to "organise" such a long and difficult expedition. But nobody ever said anything of this sort to me then, and I saw it as a long stroll rather than an expedition anyway. So I happily assumed it would all work out.

Firstly, however, my priority was money. I reckoned I would need enough to live on for about a year. I had some in savings but I would have to earn the rest, and quickly, if I was to leave by March 1st. So I took all the jobs available, working long hours, and putting aside all I could. This took up most of my time for several months, and my friends and relatives forgot all about the proposed venture during this period, probably not believing it would actually happen. But in November a number of camping and outdoor shops started their seasonal sales, and I decided that here was the chance to get everything I needed for the walk, and cheaply.

The day I bought an ultra lightweight "hooped bivi" tent, a backpack that looked as though it was made for someone twice my size, and a pair of good quality walking boots, was the day it dawned on my friends and family that I really meant to go through with this—to them—harebrained scheme.

"Good God!" said a friend. "You really mean this!"

"Oh, no," said my mother. "I thought finally you were old enough to stop doing these crazy things."

"You're out of your mind," gasped my boss of a few weeks, shaking his head and at a loss for further words. Wearing my office suit and high heels, I don't think he could begin to imagine me walking several thousand miles.

Miriam was the only person who took it all calmly.

"Great," was all she said. "Now, what help do you need? Is there anything you'd like me to do?"

With my bank balance significantly reduced and my new equipment threatening to trip me up every time I entered my tiny flat, I decided, despite being a non-planner, that the time had come to do some training. It wasn't that I was completely unfit, but in spite of telling everyone that I was an experienced hiker and had once walked for six days in the Andes (I never mentioned that it had been fifteen years previously), I hadn't done more that the occasional stroll for years. So it seemed sensible to do some weekend hikes, at least. In fact, against my own happy-go-lucky inclinations, I decided to do some Serious Training. But somehow it never actually took place. Pounding the pavements of suburbia wasn't my idea of fun; if I was going to walk I wanted to get out into the country. But this would have to be at weekends, and there were too many other things to do then.

Finally, in February, Miriam and I managed a youth hostelling weekend so that I could do a day-long training hike. It turned out to be a complete fiasco: there was heavy snow and I had to abandon the path, and I couldn't find Miriam in the village where we'd arranged to meet. Still, it proved to me I could manage fifteen miles with a backpack in adverse weather conditions. I decided it would have to do. I abandoned further training plans, saying I would get fit as I walked, starting out slowly and increasing the daily mileage when I felt I could. After all, I consoled myself, wandering minstrels didn't train, did they?

My only other attempts at planning involved trying to find ways of making or saving money while actually on the walk. Writing about the walk seemed a good bet, so I asked several newspapers and magazines if they would be interested in articles about it. Most of them said "perhaps", and wished me luck. I suspected, however, that it was merely a polite way of saying no. One national newspaper told me bluntly that they didn't think the project was at all interesting. I was about to abandon the idea of writing altogether when at last my local paper, the *Croydon Advertiser*, said they would like to receive regular reports. They didn't pay a lot, but it would help, and I accepted.

I also attempted to get sponsorship in the form of free equipment or clothes to test, or free maps. Again, however, nothing came of this except rejections and good luck wishes. It was my brother who made me realise I was going about this the wrong way.

"Nobody knows you from Adam," he told me bluntly. "They don't believe you'll do it. Wait till you're halfway round, then ask them."

I took his advice and he turned out to be right.

January 1986 arrived, and I was working at a new temporary job, my last one before the walk. One day I mentioned the proposed venture to my boss, and he was very interested. He told me his brother worked for Radio Sussex, who were based in Brighton, which coincidentally was where I planned to start walking. Could he, he asked, let his brother know about it? Without considering the possible consequences, I agreed.

Ten minutes later the consequences materialised in the form of a phone call.

"This is John Lees," said a voice. "I do the sports news for Radio Sussex. I'm very interested in your proposed walk."

"Oh, yes," I replied cautiously.

He continued: "I hold the record for walking across America; I've also walked from Land's End to John o'Groats; I'm also a centurion..."

He paused, obviously expecting some kind of reaction to this amazing revelation.

"A what?" I asked, seeing visions in my mind's eye of Roman soldiers on Brighton beach.

There was a longer pause. Then John explained slowly and carefully, as if to an idiot, that centurions were people who'd walked over a hundred miles in twenty-four hours.

"And I walked forty miles last Christmas Day," he went on. "And I ..."

At this point my brain seized up. I didn't know what to say to this man, this race walker , or marathon walker, or whatever he was. It vaguely occurred to me that he must be trying to impress me with these credentials, or prove his credibility, or something. He obviously thought I was some kind of superfit Amazonian record breaker. What had I got myself into?

"How far are you planning to walk each day?" John's question broke in on my panic stricken thoughts.

"Oh." I considered quickly; I didn't actually have a clue. "Maybe... fifteen to twenty miles."

"Is that all? John Merrill did over thirty."

Throughout the walk I was to keep hearing what John Merrill, record breaking long distance walker, had done. But at the time I hadn't even heard of him, though I wasn't about to say so.

"Oh, well," I said brightly, "I'll probably speed up later."

I had no intention of speeding up later. It didn't suit my wandering vagabond idea at all. I wanted to walk round Britain my way, taking my time, looking at the scenery and talking to people. I'd leave world-beating achievements to others who liked that sort of thing. I would be, I decided there and then, a long distance ambler.

So time rolled on, with Day 1—March 1st—getting steadily closer. I caught flu, recovered, abandoned my work, sublet my flat, wrote my first report for the *Croydon Advertiser*. Finally, on February 27th, I took the train to Brighton to stay with my cousin for a couple of nights before the start. It had begun. It was for real.

Things rarely turn out as expected, and the start of my walk was no exception. No, that is an understatement; the start of the walk was a perfect illustration of the law that if anything can go wrong, it will.

I spent most of my last pre-walk day doing last minute organising. One of the many hazards of being a non-planner is that you tend to end up with three days worth of activities to cram into the last half-day. I found that I needed a notebook to use as a diary, containers for food, spare laces for my boots; all essential items, and all taking time to get hold of. In between all this Radio Sussex phoned; they wanted to interview me. I'd never done a radio interview before, and I found the whole thing distinctly nerve-wracking, especially as I still felt inclined to lie outrageously about my reasons—or lack of them— for walking round Britain. In the afternoon I at last met John Lees, record holder, non-Roman centurion, marathon walker, and my telephone tyrant. He turned out to be friendly, encouraging, and not at all put out that I was obviously no seven foot tall Amazon with bulging calf muscles and huge strides. John's energy extended beyond long distance walking, and by the end of the day he had arranged for a representative from the local paper, plus the mayor of Brighton, to see me off the following morning. And of course Radio Sussex planned to cover the start as well.

Finally the hectic day came to an end and I went back to my cousin's house. I wanted an early night so as to be ready for the big day. But I didn't really anticipate any problems; it was all arranged. I would get up, eat a good breakfast, then get a bus from my cousin's house—three miles inland—to the Palace Pier to start the walk. The weather wasn't too bad; after all, it was just about the end of winter; tomorrow was March 1st. I fell asleep happily imagining a delightful stroll along the seafront in spring sunshine.

I awoke in the late evening, barely an hour after I'd gone to bed, with a splitting headache and stomach cramps. I felt sick and feverish, and wondered dismally what was wrong with me. Two minutes later I had to rush to the toilet, where I brought up most of the previous day's food. Owing to lack of time it had been mainly snacks—an indigestible mixture of sandwiches, salted peanuts, apples and chocolate bars. Which of them, I wondered as I crouched there shivering, had been the cause of this misery? Or was it all the rushing about and my nervousness at being on radio? Well, it hardly mattered at this point.

I returned to bed but couldn't sleep. The pounding in my head continued, and the dashes to the loo became necessary at frequent intervals, even long after I was sure nothing was left in my stomach. It became increasingly obvious as the night wore on that I had a bad case of food poisoning. What appallingly lousy timing.

By five o'clock in the morning, after a completely sleepless night, my stomach had settled somewhat and my head had cleared, but I felt desperately weak. I wasn't sure if I could walk downstairs, let alone start a five thousand mile trek. Still, having made all the preparations, I really wanted to begin if at all possible. I tried shakily to stand up. It wasn't too bad, I decided, holding on to the bed for support. I staggered downstairs, rummaged around the unfamiliar kitchen, and made myself some hot water and honey. This revived me a little, and I decided I could make it.

A few minutes later the sun rose and showed that my optimism had been somewhat premature. Three feet of snow had fallen overnight in the Brighton area. An early morning news bulletin confirmed my worst fears. There were no buses running at all; traffic was at a standstill; roads were virtually impassable. This meant if I was to leave I would have to walk the whole three miles to the pier, through thick snow. In my weakened state it seemed impossible. I decided regretfully that I would have to postpone the start of the walk.

But how could I? A moment's reflection made me realise the absolute impossibility of stopping the wheels that had been set in motion the previous day. Miriam, determined to see me off, would already be on an early morning train from Croydon. The Radio Sussex newsvan, the *Evening Argus* reporter and photographer, and the mayor, were all expected at the pier at 9.30 am. I didn't even know how I could contact them. Besides, how, after all the build-up, could I tell them I wasn't going?

I think it was my cousin's suggestion that I go home and recover in Croydon for a few days that finally decided me. I just couldn't face doing that. I had to go. So I gritted my teeth and prepared to start. After some more hot water and honey—I didn't dare eat anything—I shouldered my backpack, and instantly almost collapsed; it was far too heavy. I threw out a packet of muesli and a pair of knickers and tried again. This time I managed to stay upright and stagger out into the snow, which was deep, slippery, and very cold.

"Take it slowly," I told myself firmly, if rather shakily. "You can do it."

Still staggering under my huge weight of essential items, I ploughed on. The snow was powdery and hadn't been cleared; few people had been out that morning in what were, for Sussex, freak weather conditions. It was hard work, nothing but an endurance test. I began to wonder for the umpteenth time that morning if I could possibly give up the whole thing.

It took me nearly two hours to reach central Brighton, where I met Miriam. She, with her usual resourcefulness, had managed to catch the only train to Brighton which was running that day. Still feeling like death, with Miriam chattering brightly about the *Croydon Advertiser*'s two page spread about me, I somehow made it to the pier. in view of the Arctic conditions I was rather surprised to be met by a jovial and friendly mayor. Soon afterwards the reporter and photographer appeared, looking a little like polar explorers. And of course there was the intrepid John Lees, complete with portable recording equipment, the radio van having got stuck in the snow.

At this point I proceeded to put on the acting performance of my life. Yes, I assured them all, with a cheerful fake smile, I felt very fit. No, the snow didn't bother me in the least; no problem at all. Of course I could cope with things like that. No, my pack wasn't at all heavy. Of course I fully expected to reach Littlehampton, twenty miles away, that evening, as planned. I was a convincing liar and they all believed me. In reality I just hoped I could get out of sight of the pier before I collapsed.

Finally the interviews and photos were finished and I set off along the promenade. Miriam, the only person apart from my cousin who knew my true physical state, had decided to walk with me for a short way.

"How do you feel?" she asked with obvious concern, as soon as we were out of earshot of the crew at the pier.

"Lousy," I admitted. "I just hope I can make it to Hove."

In the end it wasn't as bad as I expected. I succeeded in walking six and a half miles of coastline that day, which at least got me out of sight of any wandering residents of Brighton. I also managed to eat and keep down some lunch, which gave me a bit more strength. However, when I reached Lancing it was snowing hard and I had had enough. A bed and breakfast proprietor, officially still closed for the winter, took one look at the weather and at me, and kindly offered to let me stay the night anyway. I gratefully collapsed, and spent the afternoon resting, recovering, and writing a *Croydon Advertiser* report. In it, I related all that had happened, but said I now felt optimistic and confident, for after such a start things could only get better. I almost believed it.

Chapter 2

The South Coast

After the frustrations of the start, the next few days went surprisingly smoothly. The second day, with my stomach virtually back to normal, though I still felt weak, I walked along the roads and seafront from Lancing to Bognor. The snow had at last stopped, though much of it still lay on the ground and the weather was very cold. I didn't meet many people; most of them were sensibly tucked up indoors by their fires. But I was recognised once; just outside Worthing a man called to me:

"Are you the woman who's walking round the whole coast of Britain?"

"Yes."

"I thought you were supposed to be in Littlehampton last night." He sounded rather smug, as though he had caught me out.

"There was a blizzard," I replied. "Didn't you notice?"

It made an excellent excuse. I shouldn't have needed one, but in spite of myself I was beginning to feel the need to live up to the super-fit Amazon image that virtually everyone else had.

But I wasn't able to, not at all. I found I was cold and tired, still weak after the food poisoning episode, and not really very fit anyway. Fifteen miles a day soon turned out to be an impossibly long way, and my pack was ridiculously heavy. The next day—the third of the walk—I pulled a muscle in my leg while walking along a three mile stretch of shingle beach above Bracklesham Bay. Walking a long way along loose shingle with a pack is a great strain on the legs, and this decided me: I absolutely had to get rid of some of my "essentials". Whatever John Merrill or anyone else could do, I was carrying too much equipment for someone my size, and clearly life would be much better if I had less to lug around.

That very night a guest house in East Wittering acquired a spare pair of socks (did I really need four pairs?), a packet of tea bags (I'd drink water), and a plastic container for eggs which had seemed a good idea when I bought it. Two days later the youth hostel warden in Portsmouth may have been surprised by the contents of a small parcel left by one of the beds: it held half a packet of macaroni, a pair of knickers, three polythene bags, a writing pad and a bottle of suntan lotion. By the next day I'd reduced my pack weight by about five pounds. It doesn't sound like a lot but it felt wonderful.

My pack also looked a little smaller, and this I found to be important for a completely different reason. When I started walking my pack looked absolutely enormous; much larger than it really was, in fact. It was actually only a 65 litre backpack, which is about average for a long hike with camping equipment, even a little on the small side. I am, however, smaller than the average person. I was also at this point in an area of the country where hikers with full equipment are rarely seen; in the Lake District or Scottish Highlands I could probably have merged into the background much more easily. Additionally, I find it more comfortable to carry my pack as high on my back as possible, which means the top of my pack was about a foot over the top of my head, giving the over-riding impression that it was taller and wider than I was myself.

The result of all this was that I looked, to most people, quite extraordinary. And I soon found that any attempt to merge into the background, even to have an ordinary chat, was doomed to failure because of this. I received a preview of what was to come on the second day, when I met a man out walking his dog, one of the few people around in the intense cold.

"Good morning," I said cheerfully.

He stared at me, appearing thoroughly bemused.

"That's a big pack you've got there."

I didn't know how to reply to this bald statement of fact.

"Er, yes," I said finally. "It's not actually as big as it looks. You see …"

He hadn't even heard me.

"I wouldn't like to carry that," he continued. "That's quite a load you've got. Hope you're not going far."

I didn't dare tell him how far I was actually going.

Soon there came another conversation, this time with a labourer on his way to work.

"Good morning."

"That's a load you've got on."

"Yes, I'm walking round the coast of Britain."

"Not with that load, you ain't. Yer'll never make it!"

He walked off, chortling to himself, before I could think of a reply. And a couple of days later, this time a friendly retired couple:

"Lovely day, isn't it?" The weather had finally cleared up.

"My goodness, what a big pack you've got there."

"Oh, I'm used to it. Nice along here, isn't it?"

"And you're not very big yourself, are you? I really don't know how you manage it. Surely you can't do that for pleasure."

It happened again and again; nobody seemed to be able to talk to me without commenting instantly on the size of my pack. It seemed there was no way I could just be an ordinary person. At first I found it annoying , later astonishing, then amusing. Finally I had to accept that I was going to be a bit of a celebrity—or a freak—while I was on this walk. I got used to the idea, though I did at times consider throwing my pack over a cliff and becoming a real wandering vagabond.

On the sixth day I arrived in Southampton. I had just walked my first hundred miles, a fact I mentioned to a sightseeing couple—in response, of course, to their comment on the size of my pack. They shared a thermos of tea with me as a celebration, sitting by the side of the river in some long-awaited spring sunshine. We chatted about the weather and my walk and their kids and all sorts of other trivia. Just for the moment I hadn't a care in the world. This was what I'd had in mind when I began the walk. And it was now going well. A hundred miles, and so far I'd had no blisters, little trouble finding my way, and overnight accommodation hadn't been a problem. I was starting to feel confident.

It was early evening and I needed to find somewhere to stay the night. However, I didn't really want to stay in Southampton itself; the youth hostel was closed that night, and I knew already from experience that it could be difficult to find accommodation in big towns without walking miles and miles. On enquiring, I was told by local people that there were plenty of places to stay in Hythe, just across the river. I had planned to go to Hythe the next day, but instead I took the last ferry over that evening.

There were indeed plenty of places to stay in Hythe. What the locals had omitted to tell me, however, was that all of them were permanently filled with workers from the oil refinery a few miles away. I walked all over town searching for a place to stay, but with no result; there was nowhere. It was the first time this had happened and I wasn't sure what to do. Finally, someone told me that the pub provided accommodation, so I went to ask. It didn't, but the barman was most interested in what I was doing. He was an ex-outward bound instructor, and a lover of walking and outdoor life. He wanted to hear all about my experiences so far, so I bought a drink and began to chat. Something would turn up concerning accommodation, I hoped, shutting my eyes to the apparent dismal reality.

Something did, though not in any way I'd anticipated. Leaning on the bar near me was a young man of the type one tends to see propping up bars in nearly every pub in the country. He looked like a fixture; he appeared to have been there since opening time and would probably stay until he was thrown out at the end of the evening. He was slightly scruffy, mildly disreputable-looking, casually dressed in an oversized roll-necked sweater and well-worn cord trousers. Probably one of the local unemployed, I thought, if I thought at all. And probably not completely to be trusted. It was the sort of snap judgement one makes almost unconsciously all the time; sometimes inaccurate, certainly unfair, but nevertheless necessary for survival in the world as it is, especially for a woman travelling alone. I was becoming used to living on my wits and trusting my instincts, and I liked to think I was pretty good at it.

The young man in question was listening to my conversation

with the barman, occasionally joining in with the odd comment or suggestion. He nodded sympathetically at my accommodation predicament, and at one point offered to drive me to one of the outlying farms to see if I could stay there overnight.

"Oh no, it's alright," I replied hastily. "I'd...I'd rather find somewhere in the town."

I noticed that he and the barman exchanged amused glances and I vaguely wondered why. But I was really more concerned about finding a place to stay; it was now getting late, the ground was becoming frosty, and I was no nearer solving the problem.

At length, with all possibilities appearing exhausted, the young man turned to me again.

"You know," he said, taking a deep drink of his latest pint. "You could always stay in the church."

I considered this. I'd never spent the night in a church before, but I wasn't averse to the idea. But I didn't want to antagonise anyone, and in spite of seeing myself as a happy wanderer, I didn't want to be arrested for vagrancy—even if it might get me a free night in a cell. But on the other hand, where else could I go? I began to voice all these thoughts at once.

"That would be OK," I said. "But I wouldn't want to upset anyone. Anyway, the church might be locked; they usually are. And shouldn't I ask the vicar or something?"

The scruffy young man took another swig of his beer. "That's alright," he replied calmly. "I am the vicar."

I began to laugh out loud, though it wasn't a particularly good joke. Then I stopped, literally in mid-laugh. For as the young man reached out to put down his glass, I could just see the tip of a clerical collar peeping out from under the neckline of his huge sweater.

"Oh," I gasped in confusion. "I...I'm sorry."

Both the barman and the vicar began to grin broadly at my embarrassment. And suddenly things began to fall into place, including the amusement over my rejection of a lift from the young man. Everything suddenly made sense if this scruffy character was indeed the vicar of Hythe.

The young vicar now proceeded to let me know his plan of action.

"Look," he said taking another swig of beer and looking at his watch all in one rapid movement. "I've got to take Compline in five minutes. Now, you come along to the church after that and I'll fix you up."

I muttered my thanks as he swiftly downed the rest of his pint and continued: "I didn't say anything for a while as I wanted to get to know you first, but I can see you're trustworthy."

Like me, he obviously went by his instincts when it came to people. But he was far better at it than I was.

Getting up to go, the vicar went on: "You know, you could do this in other places. Churches are empty at night after all. And it'll save you some money. Give my name as a reference; I'll tell the local vicar you didn't steal the silver. Where'll you be tomorrow?"

"Beaulieu," I replied. "Or possibly Lymington."

"Oh, I know the vicar of Beaulieu," my new friend replied. "Yes, nice chap; he's a friend of mine. You can stay in his church I'm sure. Just tell him the Reverend Paul Sullivan sent you. Lymington? Yes, the vicar of Lymington's a good bloke too. I'm sure he'll help you out."

While I was waiting for Compline to finish I went and bought some food from the local fish and chip shop. I told the people there about my newly found accommodation, since earlier I had asked them if they knew where I could stay. They seemed not in the least surprised.

"Oh yes," the girl said, grinning as she shovelled my chips into a bag. "Our vicar's a nice bloke. Don't worry; I bet he enjoyed that, not being recognised I mean. He likes doing things people don't expect of a vicar. When we had a sponsored walk for charity he took his dog. Got people to sponsor him for how often it peed. A p a pee, get it?"

I spent the night in the vestry of Hythe church. It had a carpet and was warm and comfortable. Rev. Sullivan arranged a way for me to get in and out, found me an electric fire, and even organised a system of extension cords so that I could have hot water.

The next day I walked to Lymington. Most of the guest houses were closed for the winter, so I took Rev. Sullivan's advice and knocked on the door of the vicarage, saying the vicar of Hythe had sent me.

"Oh," said the vicar of Lymington, obviously a little surprised. He was middle-aged and conventional-looking, everyone's idea of how a vicar should be. "Well... I suppose there's no reason why you can't stay in the church. I don't see why not, though it's never been done before. Yes... alright."

I didn't use the Church's free accommodation network again for a long time. Not wanting to impose on people, or virtually ask for sanctuary unnecessarily, I kept it for emergencies, and there weren't many. But I never forgot my night in Hythe.

On Day 10, March 10th, I reached the start of the South West Way. This is Britain's longest official footpath; from Poole in Dorset it meanders west along the south coasts of Devon and Cornwall to Lands End, then all the way through North Cornwall and North Devon to Minehead, a total distance of nearly 600 miles. Mainly following old coastguards' paths, it includes spectacular scenery and surprisingly rugged walking. It is said, by those who know, to be tougher than the Pennine Way in parts.

I had wanted to walk the South West Way for years; I expected it to be a highlight of the walk. The main reason I had decided to go round Britain clockwise was so that I could walk the South West Way near the beginning: I wanted to make sure I did it before I got bored, or broke a leg, or gave up for some other reason. So when I reached Studland, the start of the coast path, I was blindly eager to get going. This was to be my downfall.

It was a lovely sunny afternoon and I was only going as far as Swanage that day, some five miles by coast path. The weather forecast was good, so I had no worries as I climbed the steep path to "Old Harry", a large slab of rock just by the sea. I sat in the sun and took photos and chatted to some people coming in the other direction. I was so preoccupied I didn't even see the stealthily descending mist, but by the time I got to Old Harry I could barely see him. "Harry's Wife", a similar slab of rock behind, was lost to view completely. I looked up and realised for the first time that the sun was almost gone, obscured by the thickening sea mist. Still I wasn't really concerned. The path was clearly defined and signposted, and I could see quite a way in front of me. It would be alright, I was sure. I really didn't want to turn back. Not on this, my first day on the South West Way.

I began to walk along the edge of the plateau at the top of the cliff. I was right, it was fine. I met and greeted yet another pair of walkers going the other way. They were the last people I was to see for several hours.

As I carried on, the fog began to descend frighteningly quickly. In retrospect I could see that there had been warning signs, but I had been too excited to notice or heed them. At the time it honestly seemed to me that one moment it was clear and sunny and the next there was a wall of whiteness in all directions. For a while the path was so well-walked that it was passable even in fog. However, I didn't at that time realise that in many places on the South West Way the path crosses a field to a stile on the other side, and the signposts rely on one being able to see from one side of the field to the other. The first time I came to one of these was the last time. I couldn't see the other side of the field and I lost the path.

There is something uniquely terrifying about being lost in thick fog. The most alarming thing is that it is totally disorientating, mentally as well as physically, especially when one is alone. I found that the damp, blanket-like fog seemed almost to penetrate my brain, and my mind felt like cotton-wool. I had to constantly remind myself where I was, what I was doing, where I was going, to a quite ridiculous extent. Right Helen, I would say to myself firmly. You're quite safe, you're only a couple of miles from Swanage, and you've got good equipment. Now, keep calm. But in spite of reminding myself that I was not in any danger and could always put up my tent if necessary, I was close to panic at times. I would have turned back if I could, but which way was back? I didn't know, so I ploughed on, heading in the general direction of the traffic sounds, to what I hoped was Swanage.

I reached the town at last, more by luck than judgement. In my blind stumbling through the fog, I finally found myself on an exceedingly well-trodden path. This had to lead to Swanage, I thought. Where else could it go? I followed it; I had nothing to lose. And it led to a road, which I almost danced along, so grateful was I to be back in civilisation. I was indeed in Swanage, and safe. I almost hugged the first person I saw, at least until I heard his comment.

"Cor!" he said. "I thought you was a troll coming up out of the mist."

After this I was exceedingly wary of fog. The next day, at the first hint of low cloud, I had my map out to look for an escape route to the nearest road. This continued for several weeks; it was an over-reaction, but probably just as well, for the rugged terrain was proving difficult for me anyway. The South West Way was totally different from the flat countryside I had crossed so far, and it kept being proved to me that neither my map reading nor my fitness were what they should be. Climbing the steep, narrow paths with my pack left me gasping for breath and exhausted, and the knee I had hurt on the third day of the walk still gave me trouble. And I kept getting lost.

Lyme Regis was my last town in Dorset. From here to Seaton in Devon the South West Way follows a curious natural feature called "The Landslip". Throughout this stretch of coastline, portions of the cliff have eroded and slipped over hundreds of years, so that now there are very many different levels, the whole thing looking a little as though there had been a major earthquake. The strangeness is increased by the fact that the whole area is covered with dense, rain forest type vegetation. It is quite unique, and also a hard and often muddy walk—eight miles of paths, climbing and twisting through thick forest on numerous different levels. Because of the thick undergrowth it is impossible to know exactly where you are most of the time.

However, one thing is certain—you cannot get lost. I was told this countless times. It is completely impossible for anyone to lose the way on the Landslip, for there is only one path, and no way on or off except at either end. Because of this fact, numerous signs warn the casual walker to be prepared for an eight mile hike.

Well, I got lost. I never really knew how I did it, but I somehow got off the Landslip in the middle. It was impossible, they all said so, but I managed it.

How did I do it? Well, I had begun to follow the path, which was clearly defined to start with. However, as time went on it began to lose itself in the dense undergrowth. When I wasn't sure of the route I followed arrows marked on trees, as these so often mark the path on less well-defined parts of the South West Way. This had seemed to work for a while, but at length I found myself in the grounds of a huge, ornate, and utterly deserted mansion.

It is impossible to describe my feelings at being there. To put it exceptionally mildly, I was flabbergasted. This just couldn't be. There were no buildings on the Landslip, and no way off it in the middle. I actually rubbed my eyes; was I going mad, or dreaming? I honestly began to wonder if the mansion was a product of my imagination. Or had I even taken the wrong path at the start, and never even followed the Landslip? The mind can play strange tricks at times, and I was totally confused and bewildered.

Suddenly, two men came out of the mansion, workmen carrying garden tools. I breathed a sigh of relief. They were too ordinary-looking to be hallucinations, I thought. I waved a bit frantically and ran up to them.

"Where am I?" I asked.

They both began to laugh uproariously. Then they told me. It was the grounds of a boys' boarding school, and paths from the school did indeed lead into the middle of the Landslip. The arrows I had been following in fact marked the route of the school's cross-country run; they were not South West Way arrows.

I wasn't the first to make this mistake, the men told me good-humouredly. The story that it was impossible to get off the Landslip was kept up so that the school grounds didn't get invaded by hordes of walkers in the holiday season. In this way numbers of trespassers were kept down. Nevertheless, people like me turned up quite frequently, usually as bemused as I had been.

I was relieved to know I wasn't the only walker to have done the impossible. But I decided I had in any case had enough of getting lost. So from the school I walked along a minor road to Seaton, my confidence in my ability to find my way totally destroyed.

But perhaps somewhat curiously, that was the last time I lost my way for a long while. Somewhere in the confusion I must have learned to navigate, out of sheer necessity. In any event, I began to look forward to a peaceful stroll down the coast of South Devon and Cornwall. I felt sure I couldn't have any more problems ahead.

Spring comes early in Devon, and I left Exeter on March 20th in bright sunshine. I came to Torquay with the sun still shining, and the palm trees along the front looking entirely appropriate. Through Paignton and Brixham and on to Dartmouth the lovely weather continued. It was obviously summer, I decided, and the time had come to try out my new tent. I made up my mind to camp at Stoke Fleming, a few miles beyond Dartmouth. It would be the first time I'd ever camped that early in the year, but the conditions were perfect. On arrival, I knocked up the site owner, who was amazed to see someone so early in the season. However, he was happy to open the site for me, and his ten-year-old daughter was fascinated by my tiny tent. Children always loved my hooped bivi, and I ended up giving a lot of impromptu lectures on lightweight camping, and letting kids try out my tent.

Around midnight I woke up, wondering if an earthquake had hit. It hadn't; just a storm—but what a storm! Torrential rain poured down and gales raged, becoming stronger and stronger. It soon became clear I'd definitely picked the wrong night to camp. In fact I was amazed that my tent stood up to such a battering, for it often seemed as though it would blow away completely; but I checked every few minutes and it was quite secure, even waterproof. Actually I had chosen well; it was so small that it offered little wind resistance, and I found throughout the walk that it would withstand conditions in which bigger tents were blown right over.

All the same I couldn't sleep. With the deafening turmoil merely inches above me, I felt very nervous. I didn't feel able to completely trust modern camping technology, and I remained awake with adrenalin pumping through my body, listening to the storm for hours and hours.

At six o'clock in the morning, feeling quite exhausted, I peered out. The wind had dropped somewhat, but it was still raining hard and the field was flooded. How would I pack everything up and keep it dry? I temporarily solved what would be a long-term problem by zipping up the tent with everything inside it, removing the pegs, and running with the whole lot to the ladies' toilets. Here I breakfasted, shivering, on muesli and dried milk; then turned to the problem of packing up a wet tent. Since everything was now under cover, it proved not too much of a problem, until I tried to lift my pack. My knees virtually gave way, for a wet tent it at least twice as heavy as a dry one.

I struggled out into a damp, grey morning, my spirits somewhat deflated. I didn't like to admit it, but I'd had it with camping, already. This was sheer misery.

The rain continued all day. Even good waterproof clothing won't keep out that kind of rain, and by the time I reached Torcross, the next village, I was soaked. I went to the village store, bought an orange, and stood there trying to look like a customer until the pubs opened.

After a pub lunch and an unsuccessful attempt to dry my clothes I started out again, though it was still raining. At the village of Hallsands I stopped to look at the ruins of an older village down on the beach. It had been destroyed by the sea, and as I looked at the thundering breakers I could easily believe it. I also looked at the map, for earlier I had planned to walk to the youth hostel at Salcombe that day. Now, however, I didn't feel as though I could make it that far.

The only other possible place to stay was a small village just inland, called East Prawle. It was a steep climb to the village, and I didn't actually know if there would be any accommodation there, so I wasn't sure what to do.

As was often the case, it was decided for me. The rain suddenly changed to sleet, then in a moment became hail, with lumps of ice about the size of marbles. A young man nearby, who had also been looking at the ruined village, summed up the situation instantly.

"Get in the car!" he snapped at me abruptly.

I complied at once. I don't normally get in cars with strange men, but most dangers are preferable to being pounded to death by gigantic hailstones. We were joined thirty seconds later by the young man's wife, and the three of us surveyed the scene in a mixture of amazement and gloom.

"Where are you going?" the young man asked.

"East Prawle," I replied. For I'd decided; I'd go no further than I had to in this.

"Right," he said decisively, consulting his map. "I'll take you there."

"No!" I wailed loudly as he started the engine. "Stop!"

He stared at me in astonishment and I tried to explain.

"You see...I'm walking round the coast of Britain. And I have to walk; I don't take lifts."

They looked at me blankly; it sounded insane and I knew it. I tried again.

"I'm *walking*," I repeated, as though this clarified everything.

"I like it, honestly," I lied. "If...if I could just wait here till the storm eases up. It's only a couple of miles."

I finally convinced them I meant what I said, though I think they still thought I was completely mad. All the same, as the hail turned to rain again they let me out. I thanked them, apologised, and tried to explain my actions, all at the same time. Then I gave up the impossible and headed along the track to East Prawle.

Throughout the walk I found that places I visited by accident were often the most memorable. East Prawle turned out to be one of these. A tiny hamlet with one main street and a number of outlying farms, it perched on a high plateau with views down to the sea. It had friendly people, a welcoming pub, and no crowds. I was lucky to find somewhere to stay—a local couple who did bed and breakfast at an amazingly low price. I was surprised it was worth their while to bother.

"Do you get many people staying here?" I asked my hostess.

She pondered.

"Not many," she said slowly. "Now and then coast path walkers who can't make it to Salcombe."

She paused, thinking, then added: "But mainly people who are lost."

Chapter 3

Lands End and Beyond

I fell in love with Cornwall from the moment I left Plymouth and caught the ferry, which was an hour late since the ferryman had forgotten that the clocks were being moved forward for summertime. To me the coastal villages were like something out of a fairytale, with streets too narrow for cars, tiny houses crowded on top of each other along the steep streets, the whole thing looking as though it might tumble into the sea at any moment. Cawsand, Looe, Polperro—I hurried on, anxious to see what delights the next village had in store for me. And with it being only early April there weren't even any crowds to spoil things.

I was finally and belatedly getting fit. My injured leg muscle was better, my back had stopped aching from carrying my pack, and fifteen miles a day no longer seemed a complete impossibility. And I was beginning to get used to the whole venture, to take things as they came, without worrying. When I got lost on the Lizard plateau—where the paths are almost unsignposted since the Cornish County Council seems to be concerned lest one lose the feeling of being a pioneer—I wasn't frightened. I just ploughed on through gorse bushes until I found the path again. When I camped at Portscatho, where a heavy frost rendered my tent completely solid by morning, I was fascinated rather than dismayed.

Also, I no longer became defensive if people thought I was mad, or told me I was too small to do a walk like this and I'd never make it. My reaction was now more likely to be laughter than anything else. I was gaining confidence, and it showed. For having already walked a few hundred miles relatively unscathed, I could indeed consider myself a long distance walker—well, long distance ambler, anyway.

On April 12th I reached Lands End, and it's no exaggeration to say that I was quite ecstatic. I felt if I could reach Lands End then I could definitely walk round the whole coast. My friends had obviously felt the same way when I started, for I had lost count of the number of people who had seen me off with the request: "Send me a postcard from Lands End—if you get there."

It was a cold blustery day—again—as I almost danced along the coast path to the pub, souvenir and craft shop, and the famous signpost which can be seen from way down the coast. These, along with windswept rocks and pounding seas, make up Lands End.

"I've made it," I announced to the world in general, which only consisted of the few tourists who had braved the horrendous weather. "I've reached Lands End."

They looked at me as though I was quite mad. British women don't walk on coast paths alone, don't start crazy marathon walks, but, above all else, they definitely don't make announcements like this to complete strangers. But I think they rather enjoyed it all the same. Explanations followed, then congratulations, then a celebration drink at "The Lands End".

Later, still somewhat euphoric, I went to look at the craft shop. The craft workers were friendly and casually interested in what I was doing, but they put it in perspective.

At Lands End

"Walking round the coast, are you?" one man asked. "Oh yes, that's been done before. John Merrill, of course. Then there was the chap with the dog."

We are certainly a nation of animal lovers: I was always hearing about the chap with the dog.

The man continued: "Oh yes, we get em all in here. The walkers, canoeists, lots of cyclists of course; then there was that bloke with the windsurfer…"

It was beginning to sound as though there were people doing this sort of thing every day, and I found myself with a mental image of a succession of people following each other around the coast in various types of vehicle, gradually wearing a groove in the coastal paths.

I spent about an hour at Lands End. Finally I had to leave, for I was due at the youth hostel at St Just, a few miles away, where I was meeting Miriam and her daughter Yudi. We had arranged this several days ago, a complicated plan involving numerous phone calls. When would I be there? When could Miriam get away from London? It was one of four times she visited me on the walk. Other friends and relatives occasionally did the same; people enjoyed using me as an excuse to get away for the weekend. It was fun, but the logistics involved made it too complicated for me to arrange meetings very often.

In this instance everything went smoothly. We met in early afternoon and explored the area together. At sunset we walked over to Cape Cornwall, which unlike Lands End is totally uncommercialised. Followed by a stray dog, I ran all the way to the top of the high hill to watch the sunset. The dog was panting more than I was by the time we reached the top, and it was only then I realised how fit I was getting. Indeed, without my pack, I felt as though I could fly.

So, feeling like a fully fledged wandering vagabond, I left next day and "turned the corner" to the north coast of Cornwall and the long, indented west coast of Britain. It seemed like a big event. Everything was going well, and people had been really friendly. But soon after this, I was to meet the first thoroughly unfriendly person since I had started the walk. This can hardly be blamed on Cornwall, as she was not from the area. Unless, perhaps, there's something in the soil...

The village of St Agnes lies high on the cliffs of North Cornwall, in the centre of an old tin mining area, about halfway between St Ives and Newquay. On the bleak mid-April evening when I arrived it appeared to have little to recommend it, apart from the fact that it wasn't completely closed up. At this time of year most of the north Cornish villages are virtually shut for the winter, for now that the mines are closed the area survives mainly on tourism, and the tourist trade starts late in the year on this wild and windswept coast. The last two villages I'd passed through that day had both appeared almost uninhabited, their shops and hotels closed and shuttered, and I was beginning to despair of finding anywhere to eat and stay for the night. St Agnes, however, seemed to be open. It had shops and cafes, and with any luck would have bed and breakfast accommodation too. I decided to stay there.

On arrival in a place where I planned to spend the night, my routine was to check all the guest houses in order to find out which was cheapest. My budget was pretty tight, and even fifty pence more or less per night could make a lot of difference over the course of a year. So I planned to do this in St Agnes. Here, however, it looked as though I might be in luck. On the approach road to the village was a small cafe, which in its window bore the welcome sign, "B & B". It looked inexpensive, I thought. I would check. At any rate, I was hungry, and I was sure I could get a meal there.

A tired-looking woman glanced up from sweeping the floor as I entered.

"How much do you charge for bed and breakfast?" I asked.

The woman put down her broom and told me the price. It wasn't expensive, but it wasn't so cheap that I jumped at it in case someone else snapped it up. I would look around first, I decided, and I began to explain this.

"Thank you," I said as politely as I could. "But it's just a little more than I can afford. You see, I'm going to be away for a long time, so I'm on a very tight budget. I'd like to look around some more, but I may well be back if there's nothing cheaper."

It was a set speech I had tried and tested over several weeks. It made it clear I wasn't complaining about the price; I was just short of money, and therefore careful. That way I didn't upset even the most sensitive of landladies—at least I hadn't so far.

But this woman was different. A look of utter fury distorted her features as she interrupted me.

"Something cheaper!" she yelled, her previously very faint foreign inflection becoming a pronounced accent—German, I thought. "You won t find anything cheaper. You try the hotel down the road, if you want to know what things cost in this town. See what *they* charge."

She glared at me, quite beside herself. "We've no room anyway," she continued. "Out! Don't you dare come back here."

I was utterly amazed by this outburst. I tried gently to placate her; I don't like making enemies, and anyway, I did want to eat at the cafe; I was starving by this time.

"I'm not saying you're expensive," I told her. "It's just that I'm very short of money..."

But she wasn't to be calmed that easily.

"You don't know anything," she yelled. " Coming in here and saying you want it cheaper. Get out!"

I should, at this point, have just left, and in normal circumstances that is exactly what I would have done. But I had had a long day, I hadn't eaten for several hours, and I was extremely tired. I had also had a somewhat frustrating phone conversation with John Lees of Radio Sussex, during which he had almost insisted that I ring back an hour later to do a radio interview, seemingly incapable of understanding that you can't ring back when you're phoning from a deserted call box in the pouring rain. All in all, it had been a hard day, and I wasn't my usual reasonably tolerant self. So I began to lose patience.

"I'm going," I said, still speaking calmly but with my voice beginning to grate. "I only stay with *friendly* people."

My voice had begun to rise, and it rose still further with the next sentence: "In fact, I wouldn't stay here if you paid me."

This was not sensible. It merely added fuel to an already raging inferno. The woman exploded in a torrent of abuse which I couldn't match and didn't want to. Common sense prevailed, if a little late, and I headed for the door.

At this point I think a devil got hold of me. With the woman s voice still ringing in my ears, I turned and hurled at her the only insult she couldn't throw straight back—my British birth.

"Why don't you go back to your own country?" I almost shrieked. "We don't want your sort in Britain."

I didn't wait for a reply but slammed the door and ran out. There, I gulped the fresh air and stopped dead, utterly aghast as I suddenly realised what I'd just said. What on earth had made me do it? I had always prided myself on my lack of prejudice, my acceptance of everyone, my tolerance of all people regardless of their colour, race, or creed. How could I have uttered that last sentence, even in anger?

I was so appalled that even though I knew exactly how the woman would react, I contemplated going back to apologise. I really felt I'd gone too far. But at this point I heard further abuse erupting out of the doorway, and my still shakily-controlled temper erupted again.

"Don't go in there!" I yelled, ostensibly to an old couple just across the road, but actually for the benefit of the woman in the cafe who I knew would hear. "It's run by the rudest people in the whole of Cornwall."

The elderly couple—pleasant, ordinary-looking people—stared at me in amazement, and I suddenly saw the situation from their point of view. I began to laugh, albeit a bit hysterically, but it broke the tension and I calmed down.

"I'm terribly sorry," I told them. "Please forgive me."

I explained what had happened.

"Oh," the man said, looking up at the cafe. "But they're not *local* people."

This apparently explained everything, at least to a Cornishman.

"Go up to the village," he continued. "One of the locals will put you up. They'll look after you. Don't worry about *her*."

This last was said with a scornful glance at the cafe, wherein dwelt the "non-local" so unworthy even of consideration.

It was true; the locals in the village did look after me, very well indeed. I spent a restful night, and calmed down enough to see the funny side of the whole situation. Nevertheless, it was a slightly chastened happy wanderer who left St Agnes next day.

I walked right along the north Cornish coast, then on into North Devon and Somerset. I met a couple staying in a miniature castle— a folly—above the beach at Portquin. I chatted to the warden of Tintagel youth hostel, who told me of his sitting room, supposedly haunted by the victims of a mining disaster. I discussed the walk with a man from the mountain rescue team who told me how long it would take me to walk a particularly tough twelve mile stretch of coastline—he was correct to within five minutes. I made friends with the so-called "hippie convoy", a group of new age travellers who had been in the news almost continuously around this time, drinking tea with them in a field just outside Watchet in Somerset.

I left Watchet on May 2nd, and arrived in the evening at the tiny hamlet of Stolford. I was quite close to the mouth of the Severn, and already I could see the coast of Wales quite clearly. I was, I realised, nearly a fifth of the way around the coast of Britain. I began belatedly to get quite excited. All at once I realised what all the newspaper reporters and others had been on about. If I did this, if I managed to walk right round the coast, it would indeed be an incredible achievement. My imagination gripped by my awesome discovery, I sat down, yawned, changed my socks, and ate an orange. Many miles of everyday reality to go.

Before I could leave Somerset, walk up the Severn estuary, and cross over the Severn Bridge into Wales, there was one rather large obstacle to be dealt with. This was the River Parrett, a long, winding river which stretched from Bridgwater through the Somerset countryside to the sea. It had no ferries across it, no bridges seaward of Bridgwater, and was not fordable. It was also said to be fast-flowing and dangerous, almost un-navigable. So the night I arrived in Stolford I resigned myself to walking all the way upstream to Bridgwater the next day, then all the way downstream after crossing the river.

It was evening, the weather was reasonable, and I began to enquire as to where I could pitch my tent. One of the local men mentioned to me that he had an old cottage, only occupied by his daughter. It was a bit rough and ready, he said, but I was welcome to stay there. I was delighted, and agreed.

At that point I didn't know, but my host was quite a celebrity in his own right. Brendan Sellick was a fisherman, the only one in the village, who used an almost unique method of propelling himself across the mud flats to ply his trade. He had been featured in several newspapers and magazines, and I later saw further articles about him.

I heard a little about this the following morning, over a bacon and egg breakfast which Brendan insisted I eat, looking outraged at my suggestion that my usual bowl of muesli would be just fine. Over the meal I happened to mention my predicament with regard to the River Parrett. Brendan thought he had a solution; a friend of his lived in Combwich, a village right on the River Parrett, and he thought this man might be able to row me across the river. So off he went to phone and ask.

Ten minutes later Brendan returned from making two telephone calls. His friend, Bill Johnson, would be happy to take me across the River, he said. He had also contacted the local paper in Bridgwater; he hoped I didn't mind. This man, I later realised, just loved anything to do with newspapers. Anyway, it was all agreed.

I arrived in Combwich about midday to be greeted by ferryman Bill Johnson, a newspaper reporter from the *Bridgwater Mercury*, and the landlord of the local pub who invited me for a free meal. A fair proportion of the villagers seemed to be there too. For Combwich, my arrival was obviously the event of the year.

After an excellent lunch I helped Bill carry his inflatable boat down to the river. Close up the river looked quite terrifying, and I began to have doubts about the whole thing. It was nearly high tide and the river was extremely wide and fast flowing. The incoming tide was meeting the current as it flowed downstream, causing ir-regular waves and swells of a horrifyingly large size. My supposedly experienced and intrepid ferryman did little to inspire confidence either; he was a small middle-aged man with a pronounced limp. I was getting nervous, and Bill's instructions as to safety precautions did nothing to appease my fears.

"Right," he said matter-of-factly. "You'd better tie your pack to the boat. If we capsize, just make sure you stay with the boat. With the way the currents are here, we have to end up on one bank or the other."

I did as he suggested, trying not to think of the mud and cold water, what would happen to my camera and binoculars and diary, and all the other hundred and one things which would occur if we capsized. I would have to develop a belated spirit of adventure, I decided. Real travellers didn't worry about wet feet or a ruined diary. And who ever heard of a wandering minstrel trying to dry out a pair of binoculars? I smiled wanly and tried to pretend my heart was thumping from excitement rather than fear as we set off.

As Bill rowed further and further from the bank the river flowed faster, and we soon found ourselves in the middle of the waves which had so frightened me when seen from the bank. From the tiny boat they seemed even bigger, and a strong wind had sprung up which caused the boat to rock alarmingly. We seemed to be miles from either bank, out in a tiny rubber boat in the middle of nowhere.

But to my own surprise I wasn't scared any more. I seemed to have thrown all caution to the winds, and my fear along with it. In fact, I found the whole thing quite exhilarating and I began to enjoy it.

This change was mainly due to my realising, very early on, that Bill knew exactly what he was doing. I was thoroughly impressed by the way he manoeuvred his little craft, balancing the tidal flow and the current so as to steer a straight course across the river to the other bank. It was quite fascinating to watch this unprepossessing middle-aged man, who was so unexpectedly an expert sailor. I felt entirely safe in his hands, and feeling very curious, I asked him where he had learned to handle a boat like this.

Bill told me that he had had polio as a child—this accounted for his limp—and he had been unable to play the usual childhood games of football, cricket etc. So instead of feeing sorry for himself, as he easily could have done, he had spent his time messing about in boats, canoeing and rowing on the local rivers. He had in this way developed an enviable and almost unique knowledge and skill.

As I listened to Bill's story, I found myself developing a great respect for him. Although unknown outside his own area, he was a quite remarkable man.

At last we reached the other bank. Here came the hardest part, for I somehow had to stagger through the thigh-deep mud for about a hundred yards to reach dry land—not easy with a thirty-five pound pack on my back. But I finally managed it, thanked Bill profusely, and made my way to the riverside path. There, I sat down to plan my next move. I was covered from head to foot in thick mud and utterly exhausted, but quite exhilarated, and also a whole day ahead of my expected schedule.

I sat on the footpath for a while, trying in vain to remove some of the sticky mud from my clothes and hair, and looking at maps as I re-planned my route. I was amazed and delighted to realised that I was nearly at Weston-Super-Mare. From there it wasn't far at all to the Severn Estuary, then the Severn Bridge, and Wales.

There is an amusing finale to this story. Two weeks later the *Bridgwater Mercury* published an account of my crossing of the River Parrett, with a photo of Bill and me in the boat. Brendan Sellick sent my mother a copy of the article, as I had requested before leaving Stolford, and my mother read it out to me over the phone. Well, it was the last time I ever trusted a reporter to tell an accurate story. The article described my walk and my arrival in Combwich. It then went on to say the following:

"The map Helen carried showed the site of an ancient ford that was used many years ago to drive cattle across the water at low tide. Then Bill came to her rescue with the offer of a ferry service to prevent her getting wet feet."

It was a good story, but utterly untrue. My up-to-date Ordnance Survey map showed nothing of the sort. There may have been a ford there at one time, but I certainly knew nothing about it. That journalist certainly had an excellent imagination. Though in this case, I felt that the truth had been even more interesting.

Chapter 4

Wales: A Foreign Country?

On May 5th I walked across the spectacular three mile long Severn Bridge into Wales. It was quite a moment for me—well, quite an hour, anyway, since it took nearly that long. I had thought I wasn't very interested in the achievement aspect of the walk, yet as I strode along, high above the river, trying hard not to get vertigo, it really hit me. I had walked the whole of the south-west peninsula, and now I was nearly in Wales.

As soon as I reached Chepstow Youth Hostel I phoned Miriam to tell her the news.

"I'm in Wales," I announced dramatically, as soon as I heard her voice.

Either it was a bad line or her sense of humour was stranger than usual.

"What's that? You can't have; they don't come that close in to the shore. Are you sure they weren't seals? Or dolphins?"

"No! Wales, WALES," I shrieked down the line.

There was a pause.

"I know, I heard you the first time. But you're most unlikely to have seen any whales in that area."

"The country," I yelled, too agitated to be very articulate. "You know, Wales."

Light dawned at last.

"Oh, Wales!" said Miriam calmly. "Well, congratulations!"

I gave a sigh of relief.

"Now be nice to the natives," she continued jokingly. "Remember you're in a foreign country."

We both laughed, I promised to behave myself and try to learn the language, and we made plans for meeting up again. It was a memorable day.

I found the youth hostel in Chepstow, rested for a day, and when I left two days later it was raining. I stopped in a bus shelter, and there I met another walker, complete with backpack, map and boots. What he was doing in such an area wasn't clear; no doubt at first he wondered the same thing about me. But as we chatted, it turned out he had read about me in one of the walking magazines, The Great Outdoors.

"Oh," he said in surprise. "You're not at all like I expected."

I asked him what he had expected.

"I thought you'd be much bigger," he said. "And ... in a hurry."

I had been talking to him for maybe ten minutes, at most, not really very long.

"And much less friendly," he continued.

The idea of an anti-social female giant striding at speed through the Welsh countryside made me laugh. But he wasn't unique. It seemed to be hard to convince people that I just wanted to meander round Britain, and that on a wet day I'd much rather talk to someone than walk. It was a bit disconcerting to have someone say, in the middle of an interesting conversation: "Well, I mustn't keep you; you've got a long way to go." Yes, I had a long way to go, but no time limit.

Still, it was usually possible to put people right. But an incident that occurred soon afterwards—probably the most unpleasant occurrence of the whole walk—showed me that I couldn't always deal with people's preconceptions quite so easily.

I was on the north coast of the Gower peninsula, just to the south of Swansea. I had had a fairly uneventful few days before that. Miriam and Yudi had met me again at St Athan, west of Cardiff, and after that I'd walked quickly through the industrial sprawl of Port Talbot to Swansea. Then began a walk around the Gower peninsula—one of my favourite areas. Exquisite sandy bays give way to magnificent cliffs; it is yet another place where I decided I would like to live. It seemed a real pity that my memories of such a place should be marred in any way, and on my last night there as well.

In contrast to the cliffs of the south coast of Gower, the north coast is flat and marshy. The day I walked round it, the heavy rain had made the ground even wetter than usual. I had intended to camp that night but I could see it would be impossible. So when I reached the village of Crofty I decided it was time to stop. As I often did, I went to the local shop to ask if there was anywhere in the village to stay.

I had come to the wrong place. There was nowhere, neither in this village nor the next one. What was I to do?

"Is there a barn or anything I could stay in?" I asked. "Just something under cover. It's really too wet to camp."

One of the shop assistants looked at me and considered.

"Well," she said, a bit doubtfully, "I've got a shed. But it's not very nice."

I told her it would be fine, for I was in no mood to demand five-star sheds. So when she finished work for the day she drove me a mile or so inland to her house. She was right; the shed wasn't very nice—it was old and used for storage—but it was a roof over my head, and it would do. She invited me into the house for supper, and I gratefully accepted.

I was sitting at the table drinking tea and making conversation when a man in police uniform threw open the back door and burst in.

"Hello, dear," said the woman, at which I assumed the man to be her husband, and prepared to say hello to him.

The man glared at me. "Who the hell's that?" he demanded.

I couldn't think how to answer this unique greeting.

The woman explained the situation. As she did so the man continued to glower at me, circling around the kitchen to get to his seat at the table the way one circles a possibly dangerous wild animal.

"Good evening," I said nervously. Anything to break the tension.

He didn't reply for a moment. Then he asked abruptly, "What are you doing here?"

"I'm walking round the coast of Britain," I replied, trying to speak in my usual friendly fashion. "I couldn't find anywhere to stay, and it's rather wet for camping, so your wife very kindly invited me up here."

"Sleep rough, do you?" he asked, making it sound like something nasty.

"Well, not really," I replied, feeling a bit defensive in spite of myself. "I camp sometimes, in my tent. Other times I stay in guest houses or youth hostels; whatever I can find."

"Oh, I see, of no fixed abode, then, are you?" he asked, now looking at me as though I were some sort of worm which had crawled up out of the ground. He paused. "You haven't committed a murder or anything, have you?" he asked.

I honestly thought he must be joking. I nearly told him I'd committed half a dozen murders, but it's just as well I didn't, as it turned out.

"You can check with Croydon Police Station if you like," I told him, smiling. "I used to go there to self-defence courses. They might remember me."

"Right!" he said, deadly serious. "I will. I'll see if you've got a record."

I couldn't believe it. It suddenly dawned on me that this man really believed I was a crook, simply because I was walking round Britain. Like most honest people, I feel uncomfortable when treated like a criminal. I didn't like the situation at all. I wanted to leave, now! However, the policeman's wife was at this moment getting the supper ready and chatting politely. I really didn't see how I could go without being very rude to her. So, feeling most unhappy, I stayed where I was.

Supper was a miserable meal. It was eaten almost in silence, with even the woman finally giving up all attempts at friendly conversation, and the man every so often firing questions at me as though it were a police interrogation. My answers appeared to confirm his suspicions—I wasn't living in one place, I didn't have a job, I was walking and camping—therefore, in his eyes, I was a criminal.

At long last the meal was finished. It was clear to all concerned that I couldn't possibly stay there the night under the circumstances. Tentatively I asked the woman if she could give me a lift back to the village, and she agreed. Shouldering my pack again, I restrained the impulse to be thoroughly rude to her husband, to tell him exactly what I thought of him. He deserved it. But his wife didn't, and anyway, apart from making me feel better it wouldn't achieve anything.

Nevertheless, I couldn't hold myself back from being thoroughly sarcastic. I thanked him profusely for his hospitality, and told him I was quite sure Croydon Police Station would be delighted to hear from him. Would he like me to give him their phone number, I asked. But it was all wasted on this man, who merely told me again that he'd check up on me in the morning.

The woman was extremely apologetic on the way back to the village, while I was silent with disbelief. How could this have happened? Everyone else treated me like a celebrity.

In the end the day finished happily. On the outskirts of Crofty, with rain still falling, I found a motel. It was officially closed until the summer, but the proprietor very kindly offered to let me stay at no charge. His kindness and hospitality restored my faith in human nature, and later, drying my clothes by a roaring fire, I thought over the events of the day and vowed not to let them undermine my trust in the human race as a whole.

Over the next few days I walked through the more industrial areas surrounding Llanelli, took a long detour round the estuaries of the rivers Towy and Taf (I tried to get a ferry across these but had no luck), and did a quick tour of Laugharne, of Dylan Thomas fame. Most of the walking was on roads, or footpaths which ended abruptly at barbed wire fences or similar, so I was immensely relieved when I reached Pembrokeshire and found myself back in official walking country. For the Pembrokeshire Coast Path is another Long Distance Footpath, stretching for approximately 180 miles around this south-west corner of the Welsh coast. This meant that, with luck, the footpath would continue all the way round the coast. This was honestly becoming rather unusual—and I had bruises and scratches to prove it. Either the footpaths were marked on the map but showed no sign of existence on the ground, or they had been obstructed by a barbed wire fence, a ploughed field, or some other insurmountable obstacle. By law a public footpath has to be kept open and accessible; one is not allowed to plough it up, fence it off, or otherwise obstruct it. Yet all too often this is done. The Ramblers Association has virtually declared war on footpath-destroying landowners, and they work hard to keep all footpaths open and accessible. Meanwhile the farmers complain that they have to keep open paths the public never use, while the walkers complain they can t use them because they can't find them.

The advantage of Long Distance Footpaths is that they are well-walked and regularly maintained. This was certainly the case on most of the Pembrokeshire Coast Path. The first section, from Amroth to Tenby and then west along the coast, was clearly marked and easy to follow. The only difficulty was a Ministry of Defence rifle range, which necessitated a long detour. The first footpath-type problem didn't occur until close to the village of Angle. Here the path goes so close to the edge of the cliff I felt as though I was going to fall into the sea. Indeed, it looked as though the farmer had placed his fence as near the edge as was legally permissible. I suspect this is in fact the case, but it makes for an interesting walk!

In Tenby an amusing incident occurred, one which had me giggling for weeks afterwards. I had taken a day off, and decided to visit Caldey Island, just off the coast. The Cistercian monastery on this island has daily tours, but only for men. This was very frustrating, but suddenly I had an idea. Throughout the walk I had often been mistaken for a teenage boy; I had my hair very short and old army trousers weren't everyone's idea of feminine attire. Perhaps, I thought, I could put this to good use. Maybe I could join the tour.

I could and I did. Nobody challenged me, though I suspected I was getting one or two rather odd looks. But nobody would really believe that a woman would blatantly try to pass herself off as a man in this way, so they saw what they expected—a boy. And anyway, I thought, how would they check? Who would dare say to a somewhat effeminate-looking teenage boy in rather butch ex-army clothes: "Excuse me, are you really male?" So I enjoyed the tour, and perhaps the deception even more.

From Angle the coast path traversed the whole of Milford Haven. This is an area many walkers miss out, especially if they are short of time, which is a pity, for this section is one of the most unusual walks in the whole country. The path follows a circuitous route through oil refineries, farmland, and industrial areas, and every effort has been made to make it interesting. To my mind it certainly succeeds, though it is very different from the usual country walk. At one point you may be walking along a vegetation-lined track, feeling as though you are in the depths of the country; then, without warning, the path will suddenly go right under a jetty, pass over the top of a pipeline, or skirt the edge of an oil refinery. It really keeps you guessing.

The next section of the Pembrokeshire Coast Path is bisected by two rivers. These are both quite small, and can be easily crossed if the tide is low enough; one by stepping stones and the other by wading. However, since there is a three hour walk between them the timing is a problem—how does one make sure of reaching both at low tide? It is difficult, but with a bit of careful organising I managed it, splashing across the second river at high speed just ahead of the incoming tide.

The rest of the 180 mile path was a delight, with picture postcard views and few real difficulties. I didn't get lost, and there were no problems with freak hailstorms or other hazards. Yet it was here that I encountered another potential danger—dogs. The incident in question occurred on a stretch where I had very slightly lost my way. I wasn't too worried, as I could see the sea, and the terrain was flat and walking therefore easy. I wasn't even very concerned when I found myself crossing someone's back garden—people very rarely minded. However, as I rounded the next bend I stopped dead, my heart in my mouth, as I almost fell over four enormous mastiffs who were snoozing by their front door. At the same moment the dogs awoke. They leaped up, turning in an instant into guard dogs intent on protecting their property, and began to bark ferociously.

I was so frightened that I became absolutely calm. It is a state I have noticed only occurs in a real emergency—but that is what I felt this was. I began to back away, very slowly, breathing deeply and trying not to show panic.

"Nice doggies," I told the huge monsters, in what I hoped was a soothing tone. "I'm just going, it's alright."

I hoped they believed me as I groped desperately behind me; where was the gate?

At this point, a white-haired old man appeared around the corner, obviously the owner of both the property and the dogs. I must have looked as shaken as I felt, for he became extremely worried and contrite, and he called the dogs off at once. Immediately they left off barking at me and metamorphosed into enormous lapdogs, fawning and wagging their tails. I almost collapsed with relief.

The man insisted I sit down and drink some water to recover, and I was in no state to raise too many objections. Now that I knew I was safe the shock had hit me, and I couldn't stop shaking.

I stayed and chatted to the man for quite a while, with his big dogs now licking my feet and treating me as an old friend. Their owner told me they were actually quite harmless, but since he lived on his own he kept them for protection. After all, he remarked, no-one would try to take on four mastiffs. I silently agreed!

At last, on May 31st, exactly three months after I left Brighton, I reached Poppit Sands Youth Hostel, near Cardigan. This was the end of the Pembrokeshire Coast Path. Here I crossed the river, courtesy of a friendly fisherman with a boat, and began to walk up the coast of mid-Wales. Typically, a fair proportion of my first day was spent climbing the barbed wire fences of a blocked-off path. Perhaps I should have been able to predict this by now, I thought, as I balanced precariously on top of one of the fences. At any rate, I hoped it wasn't a taste of what was to come.

As I journeyed up the coast of mid-Wales I felt more and more as though I was in a foreign country. In Pembrokeshire the differences between England and Wales hadn't been all that obvious, since there is a lot of English influence in that part of Wales. But from New Quay to Aberaeron and on up to Aberystwyth one was very obviously in the real Wales. Cymru, land of song, some call it. But for me at that time, it was the land of unpronounceable names. The Welsh language at first seemed like an insurmountable problem. How could I ask for directions when presented with a name which appeared as a long collection of unconnected letters, defying all attempts to form a coherent whole, and possibly without a single vowel? How, I would ask myself as I stared at the map, should I pronounce Cwmtudu, Llanrhystud, or Machynlleth?

Then there were the Welsh signposts. Theoretically, all signs and notices in Wales must be in both English and Welsh. However, in country areas sometimes one language will be left off, and in remote areas it's often English.

This caused some highly amusing incidents. During one period of several days I kept seeing signs pointing to a place called Llwybr Cyhoeddus. It must be an extremely important place, I thought. There were so many ways to it, and even paths across fields directed one to it. It must, I thought, be a place of some historical or other interest. I decided that I would go there, but I just couldn't find it anywhere on the map. It was very puzzling, but eventually I found out why. Llwybr Cyhoeddus means "public footpath" in Welsh.

At last I hit on a solution to the language difficulties. Since I reckoned I would be in Wales for roughly another three weeks, I decided I still had time to learn the language. It couldn't be that difficult, and I thought I could at least memorise the rules for pronunciation, and maybe a few simple words or greetings, if nothing more. And that way I'd have no more misunderstandings like the Llwybr Cyhoeddus one.

Having made up my mind, I acquired a small book which

professed to teach Welsh painlessly by means of cartoons. This sounded like a wonderful idea and I was quite enthusiastic about the whole venture. That evening the first thing I did was to turn to the page on pronunciation. The book assured me that Welsh pronunciation was easy, as it was completely regular. This is true, but what the book didn't mention was that, regular or not, some of the sounds were almost impossible for an unpractised English person like me to get her tongue around without a teacher to show me how it was done. The 'double L' sound was the hardest, and when it occurred twice in the same word, as for instance in the towns Llanelli and Llangollen, it reduced me to a spluttering wreck.

Still, my early attempts at correct pronunciation, bad as they were, had one good result—the local people were delighted. This spurred me to continue trying to learn the language. After all, my cartoon book assured me that it would be painless. But it wasn't, and I never managed it at that time. The grammar and irregularities defeated me, to say nothing of the fact that after a day's walk I was usually tired out, and would fall asleep over my cartoon book. I had had grandiose ideas about getting my book out at lunchtime in a Welsh pub so that the locals could help me, but it never happened. Either I was too busy eating, drinking and talking, or my book was buried somewhere inside numerous plastic bags to protect it from the elements.

I gave up learning Welsh one evening when I was foolish enough to look on at later chapters of the book. I came to the one on mutations, which is the name for the curious—to the English—habit words have of changing their first letter, depending on what word comes before them. There were, the book said, twenty-seven rules for when mutations occurred. That was it, I decided. I was giving up Welsh. I thought it was time for a purge of my surplus equipment, and my cartoon book was unnecessary and probably weighed an extra half pound. And so a north Wales guest house acquired a Welsh language cartoon book for its next guest.

My Welsh pronunciation, however, did improve significantly as the weeks went by. Later on I took a trip to the place with the longest name in Wales, Llanfairpwllgwyngyllgogerychwyrndrobwll-llan-tysiliogogogoch, known locally and more conveniently as Llanfair P.G. Encouraged by my earlier efforts, I decided I was going to learn to pronounce this name, and it turned out that one of the local souvenir shops had a record to teach people to do just this. This song went through the whole thing, syllable by syllable, with a catchy tune to help. I stayed in the shop for about half an hour, and by the time I left I was word perfect—or do I mean syllable perfect—and childishly delighted at having learned the name.

There is, however, much more to Wales than simply a strange language. Here, for the first time, I found long sandy beaches, often stretching for several miles. I had wanted to walk along beaches ever since the start of the walk. My imagination had conjured up visions of strolling for miles along the shore in bright sunshine. This had never happened. Firstly, Britain has very few sandy beaches, most of the coastline being rocky, stony, or a mixture of small sandy bays and unscalable cliffs. It is even more deficient in bright sunshine, or had been in the early months of 1986. But in Wales, at last, I had some sunny weather, and this coincided with my reaching some of the long sandy beaches of mid-Wales. So I walked on the beach northwards from Borth most of the way to Tywyn—apart from a ferry crossing—and then from Barmouth to Shell Island. This last—an eight mile stretch—was the longest for many months, and wasn't to be beaten until I reached the sandy beaches of north-east Scotland.

Then there were some memorable towns and villages. I was delighted to see a dolphin at New Quay, and seals at Cwmtudu. Aberystwyth became one of my favourite cities. And Machynlleth, which I visited on a detour inland, was added to the list of places in which I would like to live.

Then came Portmeirion, appearing suddenly out of the mist like something out of a fairytale. I phoned Miriam from there; I knew she loved the place, and I wanted to tell her that I had fallen under its spell too. And soon after this I began to walk around the curve of the Lleyn peninsula, that piece of north Wales that stretches westwards from Porthmadog, an area of cliffs, sandy beaches, and secluded coves.

Unfortunately at this point the weather changed for the worse, turning to rain, wind and fog, all at the same time. The day I reached Criccieth there were gigantic waves washing right over the main road along the seafront, and as I continued the weather became even worse. I stayed overnight in a small village, and the next day I set off for Abersoch, near the tip of the peninsula, in really appalling conditions. It was intensely depressing. Abersoch is a sailing centre—described to me by someone in Pwllheli as a "grotty, yachty place". It is the sort of town that is delightful in good weather, but utterly dismal during the sort of conditions I was experiencing. In fact, this was true for the whole of the Lleyn peninsula. I realised I'd had enough of it; I really didn't want to go to Abersoch. I wanted to head east, back to the towns and cities of north Wales. As I walked through the rain, I found I was saying to myself, over and over again, "I don't want to go to Abersoch. I don't want to go to Abersoch."

I stopped abruptly in my tracks. "Hell," I thought suddenly, "Then don't go! You don't have to."

So I didn't. I cut across the middle of the Lleyn peninsula to Nefyn and then began to head east again. I felt very relieved and much happier. It was the biggest "short cut" I had yet made, and it had taken quite a lot of effort to drag myself away from the coast. In theory I didn't have to stick to the coast if I didn't want to; I made the rules, if there were any. But, in spite of knowing this, I had somehow got locked into a particular way of looking at things, of assuming I would keep at least reasonably close to the sea. But I didn't have to; I was free to go wherever I wanted. This was the idea of the trip, and in this case it probably saved me from a bout of pneumonia.

My short cut brought me closer to Wales' north coast, and soon I was walking through Caernarfon, with its huge castle, and next day I reached Bangor. I began to realise I was nearly out of Wales, and I had now walked over 1,500 miles. This was hard to believe, for I had done it in relatively easy stages, and I really didn't feel as though I had walked that far. After the first month, which had admittedly been more painful than pleasurable, the walking had been quite easy; it is amazing what can be achieved if one simply keeps going at a steady pace. I kept looking at myself, expecting to look or feel different. I mean, 1,500 miles was something of a marathon, wasn't it? I ought to look superfit, lean and brown and muscular and obviously different from the rest of the human race. But the face and body which stared back from the mirror looked supremely ordinary. I obviously wasn't going to metamorphose into anything special.

I finally reached Llandudno in mid-June. This was the first large holiday resort I had walked through since the tourist season had started, and it gave me a taste of what was to come in these places as the summer continued. From one end of the town to the other I had to run the gauntlet of stares, nudges, and continual cries of "That's a big pack you've got there", always from people who thought they'd just made a most original and unique comment. I often found myself wishing I could ditch my pack and just be an anonymous holiday-maker for a while, and later on, in similar places, I began to do just that.

Then at last I was walking up the estuary of the River Dee, over the bridge at Queensferry, and back into England. I had walked the whole coast of Wales. When I reached Parkgate, the first village on the Wirral peninsula, I was amazed to be given a rousing welcome, and treated like an old friend. After a cup of tea, a long chat, and a promise to send a postcard when I reached Brighton, I was off again. My next stop was Liverpool. Then would come Cumbria, and soon—amazingly soon—I would be in Scotland.

Chapter 5

North-West England

From the centre of Liverpool I walked through a seemingly end-less stretch of dockland, though in reality it was only about five miles. Soon I reached Formby; then came a stretch of wide sandy beach to Southport, followed by a long trek up the River Ribble to Preston. This had the distinction of being the longest day of the whole walk, mileage-wise, for by the time I arrived in Preston I had walked thirty miles. I was utterly exhausted and went straight to bed, vowing never to walk that far again. These people who can do thirty or forty miles a day, every day, are obviously a different species, I decided.

Soon Blackpool's famous tower loomed up in front of me. Once there I decided to learn from my experiences in Llandudno, and I found somewhere to leave my pack so that I could be a tourist for a few hours. I joined the holiday-makers at Pleasure Beach, went on the Big Dipper and other white knuckle rides, and generally had a lot of fun. Most walkers and countryside-lovers threw up their hands in horror when I told them, but I loved Blackpool.

Next came Lancaster and Morecambe, and then the Area of Out-standing Natural Beauty at Silverdale. From the shores here I could see across to the beaches of Cumbria, with the hills of the Lake District towering behind. In between lay the wide sweeping curve of Morecambe Bay, which somehow had to be negotiated.

Morecambe Bay stretches from near Heysham in Lancashire, all the way round in a wide arc almost to Barrow-in-Furness in Cumbria. At its widest point it must be at least ten miles across, and its total area is enormous. At high tide the sea completely fills it, while at low tide it goes out for several miles, leaving an expanse of golden sand as far as the eye can see in all directions. The sand looks deceptively safe, but is actually extremely dangerous, for there are large, shifting areas of quicksand, said to have swallowed tractors without trace. The tide is equally treacherous, for it comes in incredibly quickly: "faster than a galloping horse," say the locals. In fact it is a tidal bore—a wave which travels down the whole length of the bay twice a day. The bore is popular with dare-devil surfers and canoeists, but exceedingly dangerous for the unwary swimmer or holidaymaker, who can be swept away before realising what has happened. For this reason there are numerous warning signs on all the beaches telling people to beware of the tide, and a siren is sounded half an hour before high tide each day to warn people to leave the shores. Yet still the coastguard service has its hands full in summer, rescuing people who have been lulled into a false sense of security by the safe-looking miles of sandy beach.

In former times it was possible to walk from Lancashire to Cumbria across Morecambe Sands. Indeed, in the last century and earlier this was the traditional route to Cumbria, and often the only route. There are still rights of way marked on Ordnance Survey maps, although a note on the map warns that these may be dangerous. This is an understatement; it is absolutely suicidal to attempt to cross the sands without a competent guide, of whom there are few left.

I very much wanted to walk across the sands of Morecambe Bay. On a walk round Britain it seemed the most appropriate route to take, following the traditional way of hundreds of years. Also, I didn't like walking round estuaries and bays; I'd had enough of them. However, being swallowed up by quicksands, or drowned by the incoming tide, wasn't my idea of fun. So, having been warned off by the locals, I had regretfully decided to give up the idea. But when I arrived at Arnside Youth Hostel I discovered my usual good luck was still holding. One of the few guided walks was due to take place the very next day. The hostel warden gave me the details, and I phoned Cedric Robinson, the guide. Yes, he said, I could come.

Next day, I left my pack at the Youth Hostel, and set off for Silverdale, where the walk was starting. I planned to return by train after the

The Crossing of Morecombe Bay

walk, collect my pack, and go back again by train to the point at which I had finished walking. This meant I wouldn't have to carry my pack over the sands. Pointless, some people told me, while others said it was cheating. But it gave me a chance to do this once in a lifetime walk unencumbered.

Accompanying me was Julie, the assistant hostel warden, who was in dire need of a day off. Something of a workaholic, she had finally been prised away from her endless round of cooking and sweeping, and ordered to join me and have fun. Neither Julie nor I were quite sure where the walk started from, but we needn't have worried; all we had to do was follow the crowds. For it seemed as though the whole of Lancashire must be going on this walk, and there must have been several hundred people who eventually congregated down by the shore at Silverdale.

As we waited in the sunshine Julie and I studied the gathering throng and tried to guess who our guide might be. Which one of these people would be competent to lead a huge crowd across the notoriously dangerous sands?

"It must be him," I suggested, as a tough, fit-looking young man in shorts and hiking boots, map in hand, arrived. But no, he was just another tourist.

"I bet that's the one," said Julie confidently, pointing to a workmanlike fellow in thigh boots and waterproof jacket. But again, she was mistaken.

We scarcely noticed the arrival of a small, inconspicuous-looking figure, perhaps in his late fifties. He had a tanned, weather-beaten face, suggestive of a life spent outdoors, but looked otherwise fairly ordinary. He was probably retired, and a keen walker or bird-watcher, I thought as I looked at him, rejecting him instantly as a possible leader of the walk. Now which one was our guide? Perhaps it was this next man; he looked like a local ...

"Could everyone listen a minute."

A voice—quiet yet firm and carrying—brought us all to attention, and Julie and I stared in surprise. It was the small, unassuming-looking man I had noticed earlier.

"I'm Cedric Robinson, your guide," continued the quiet voice. "I'll be leading this walk."

So this was Cedric Robinson, fisherman and guide, the famous "Sand-pilot" of Morecambe Bay, and author of several books. I wouldn't have believed it.

As our guide spoke, the crowd gathered closer and listened. Cedric said a few words to us about following his instructions and keeping away from the quicksands; then he set out across the bay and the crowd followed.

As the great throng of people stopped their talking and milling about, and began to follow this one unassuming-looking figure, the walk seemed to take on an almost biblical quality. Indeed, it reminded me—perhaps a little fancifully—of accounts of the crossing of the Red Sea. For there they all were—young and old, male and female; families, single people, dogs, babies—all stretching out in a procession of perhaps half a mile in length. All of them placing their trust—indeed, quite literally their lives—in the hands of this one unlikely looking man. I wondered if we were all quite mad. Though indeed, I had to admit that our guide did make quite a convincing modern day Moses after all, as he strode out confidently, hair flying in the wind, stick held firmly in his hand. He obviously knew his stuff. Small though he was, he appeared larger than life, and I fancied I could almost hear him saying: "Arise, and I will lead thee to Grange-over-Sands."

Led by Cedric, the procession followed a decidedly zigzag course, designed to avoid the deepest pools of water and any areas of quicksand. We walked for several hours, at times over firm sand, then through knee deep pools, the latter to the delight of the children on the walk. Twice, of necessity, we passed close to the quicksands. When this occurred Cedric insisted that the straggling crowd keep together; he then divided them so that they could cross in two separate groups under his watchful eye. His calm way of handling the crowd was most effective and impressive. Despite his apparent ordinariness he was obviously a natural leader. I found myself fascinated by the man, and I left Julie so that I could try to worm my way to the front of the crowd and talk to him. I found our guide alone at the front of the procession, and I introduced myself. He remembered our phone conversation—there weren't too many round Britain walkers on this walk—and seemed happy to answer my questions. How, I asked, did he know the route so well?

Cedric pondered a moment. "Well," he said slowly, "I've been a fisherman all me life, and me father and grandfather before me."

He then told me how he had grown up and lived all his life on Morecambe Bay, so that he knew the sands in the way a stranger never could. Thus he could recognise signs, small changes invisible to other people, which would tell him the state of the tides and the sands. Yet still, to be absolutely sure, he checked and re-checked the proposed route before each guided walk, looking out for last minute shifts of the treacherous quicksands, making certain the route was safe. As he talked I became more and more convinced—if I hadn't been already—that we had a first-rate guide, a man truly deserving of his title "The Sand-pilot".

After about three hours walking we finally reached Kents Bank, near Grange-over-Sands, in Cumbria. Julie and I collected our certificates stating that we had walked across Morecambe Bay; we then washed our feet and caught the train back to Arnside Youth Hostel. I would return by train to Kents Bank to continue the walk next day.

Back at the village of Arnside, we sat in safety above the railway viaduct and watched the tide come in. As the spectacular tidal bore thundered down the length of the bay and crashed against the wall of the viaduct below us, I shuddered at the thought of being caught by it unawares. It made me grateful for Cedric Robinson and his knowledge of Morecambe Bay. It is unfortunate that he is one of the last of his kind; few of the younger generation know the sands as he does, and soon there may no longer be any sand-pilots.

So ended a day never to be forgotten. Next morning I bid a final farewell to Lancashire, returned to Kents Bank, and began to walk up the coast of Cumbria. I had now walked, in all, close to 2,000 miles, and I was over a third of the way around the coast of Britain.

One of the sights I was interested in seeing in Cumbria was Sellafield Power Station. I would pass quite close to it, and I was most interested in finding out about it, and also what local people thought of it. I hoped very much that I could perhaps visit it too. Well, a visit was easy enough, I discovered. But finding out about it? I didn't realise just how difficult this was to be.

A few miles from Sellafield I reached the village of Seascale, and here I stopped, bought a cup of coffee, and chatted to a few local people. It wasn't too hard to bring the subject round to nuclear power stations, since the village was right next door to one, and consequently everyone had opinions about Sellafield. However, these opinions weren't in the least consistent.

"Oh it's just fine," one woman told me. "There's no danger, no problem at all."

This may have been true, but it turned out her husband had been unemployed until he found work at the power station, so she was hardly unbiased.

The next person I met told me gloomily, "This place used to get lots of tourists. But they don't come here any more, not with that place so close."

The truth is that some of the tourists may have been put off, but in fact the power station probably attracts more sightseers than the scenery ever did.

Then I was told, by an emotional, angry young woman: "It's destroying the vegetation. You go there and see. Nothing grows there any more."

I did go, and I did see. The vegetation certainly hadn't been destroyed; all the plants looked healthy and thriving. They could have been radioactive for all I knew, but they certainly weren't obviously damaged in any way.

I began to realise that with such an emotive subject it was going to be difficult to find out anything for certain. So I decided the only thing to do was to see the place for myself. There was a visitor centre at Sellafield, and they arranged coach tours of the actual site. I decided I would go on one, and later that day I walked the two miles from the coast to the main entrance to the nuclear power station.

I was quite impressed by the well-organised exhibitions at the visitor centre, and as I browsed around I found myself really looking forward to the tour. Everyone at the centre was very open and friendly, security appeared to be minimal, and everything was proceeding in a calm, relaxed fashion. That is, until our tour guide asked if we had any final questions before we entered the site.

At this point I remembered something. I had a camera with me on this walk, an Olympus XA, which was small enough to fit into my pocket and be carried everywhere. I had actually forgotten I had it with me, but it would be really nice to get some photos, actually inside the power station. I wondered if I could. I realised I had better check, so in all innocence I asked: "Is it alright to take photos from the coach?"

I wasn't at all prepared for the response, although in retrospect I can see perhaps I should have been. The guide looked as though he was about to have a fit. Completely unknowingly, I had been about to break one of the strictest rules of Sellafield—cameras were definitely not allowed inside. Visitors who had been carrying cameras had been told this, individually and unobtrusively, in advance. All of them, that is, except me, for since my camera was so small and was hidden in my pocket nobody had even realised I had it with me. The guide tried visibly to keep calm as he explained the situation to me. Perhaps his job was at stake; at any rate, he seemed extremely relieved when I handed over my camera with no argument, to be collected after the tour.

After this bit of excitement the tour was actually rather boring. If there were any great secrets to be illicitly photographed, I didn't see them. Still, everyone tried hard; the guide worked at explaining how the power station operated, trying to make the whole thing accessible to non-scientists. It was interesting just to have been there, and I was glad I had come. Indeed, the only disquieting incident had been the concern over my camera.

Back at the visitor centre, however, even my uneasiness about this was quickly dispelled as we were given the chance to ask questions about the centre or about nuclear power in general. The Chernobyl disaster had taken place some weeks before, and I asked several reasonably searching questions about the precautions taken at Sellafield to ensure a similar incident couldn't happen there. While I couldn't follow all the technical details, the reply convinced me that great care was taken over safety, that the people involved in the running of Sellafield were not ogres out to destroy our planet, but reasonable people doing the best they could. By the time I left I was quite impressed overall. I had found the people who worked at Sellafield much more convincing than the overemotional anti-any-thing-nuclear-whatsoever types, like the woman who had told me the vegetation could be seen to be dying when it quite clearly wasn't. For in spite of trying to have an open mind, I had had severe doubts about nuclear power beforehand, partly because of the rather sinister-looking sight a large nuclear power station presents. Now, having seen round one and talked to its workers, my doubts were well on the way to being dispelled.

However, this feeling didn't last long, for it turned out that nothing is quite that simple. A couple of days later I became involved in another discussion on nuclear power, and related my recent experiences to the warden of the youth hostel where I was staying at the time. He looked at me as though I was some kind of gullible idiot.

"Of course they're convincing," he said, somewhat cynically. "They're trained to be. I bet they didn't tell you they had to close the beach at St Bees three times this year, did they?"

"No they didn't," I replied, feeling a bit sheepish at my apparent gullibility. "Why did they do that?"

"Because there were leaks, of course," replied the warden. "But of course they don't tell you that on the tour; it just gets hushed up. There've been lots of leaks, but of course they just tell you what they want you to hear. That whole tour's a waste of time; it's just an exercise in public relations for British Nuclear Fuels."

Perhaps because I had been so convinced before, my disillusionment was absolute. I was disgusted with myself for being taken in by the calm, rational people I'd met at Sellafield, simply because they spoke convincingly. I'd believed them, just like that.

This feeling continued until several weeks later, when I happened to meet a woman who had once worked at Sellafield. She shed new light on the picture, yet again.

"Yes," she said, "They do close the beach at St Bees quite often. They need to test the levels of radiation there. It's one of their regular safety checks, and they have to close the beach while they do it. It has nothing to do with leaks."

Who was I to believe? I didn't know any more. And my confusion was compounded when I recounted this continuing saga to yet another ex-power station worker. He sighed, before telling me:

"They do close it to test; that's quite true. But there have been leaks as well, quite a number of them, and they do keep quiet when anything like that occurs."

This whole matter was getting unbelievably complicated—a web of intrigue, lying and manipulation which was very disquieting to say the least. How does one find out the real truth, I wondered? About this, or anything else for that matter? Who can you believe? I knew from my own experiences that one couldn't believe anything the newspapers said—several had interviewed me about my walk and then printed what amounted to absolute fiction, sometimes attributing long quotes to me of which I had uttered not one word. Now I had been told totally conflicting "facts" about Sellafield by supposed experts, by people who'd worked there, by locals—who was right? Perhaps, I thought rather despairingly, the doctor I had met at Ravenglass was correct when he told me that nobody actually had the whole picture; for to do so one person would have to have a detailed knowledge of nuclear physics, biology, medicine, economics, and several other disciplines, all at the same time. If he is right it's rather alarming.

So I finished the walk with no clear conclusions about nuclear power stations. In fact, my searching taught me a lot more about people than it did about nuclear power. I did find myself wishing that power stations weren't so often built on such beautiful stretches of coastline, but I had to admit that they were extremely interesting places to visit. Beyond this, however, I just didn't know—I couldn't begin to untangle the half-truths, emotional reactions, and political manipulation which surrounded anything to do with nuclear power.

In Cumbria I succeeded in solving one other major problem: the fact that after 2000 miles my boots were beginning to wear out. I really had to get new ones, and at this point I remembered my brother's words, way back in February: "Wait until you're halfway round, then ask them." Well, I wasn't quite halfway, but it was worth a try.

The manufacturers of my boots were based quite nearby, so I wrote to them explaining the situation. A few days later, not expecting very much, I followed up this letter with a phone call.

The marketing manager of the company had just returned from a continental holiday, a fact which rapidly became obvious. She hadn't had time to read my letter, and in fact sounded as though half of her brain was still on the Costa Blanca or somewhere similar.

"Oh...yes," she stammered in response to my query. "Well...I'm sure we have your letter somewhere. The boots wore out, did you say? After 2000 miles? They should have lasted longer than that."

She didn't sound as though she was sure whether I was complaining that the boots had worn out and asking for a replacement pair, or asking for sponsorship. I didn't enlighten her, as actually I wasn't quite sure myself. I hadn't made this kind of request very often; I wasn't certain of the rules.

"Well... I'm sure we can send you some more," continued the marketing manager, obviously thinking out loud. "Yes. OK. What size do you take, and where should I send them?"

And that was all there was to it. A brand new pair of boots were duly sent for me to pick up in Carlisle, along with a request for regular reports on their progress and photos of me wearing them. Some months later I found that a quote from one of my reports was included in the company's latest advertisement, describing me as "Helen Krasner—Round the Coast of Britain Walker". After 2000 miles it seemed as though everyone was prepared to take me seriously.

Chapter 6

South-West Scotland

I crossed the border into Scotland on July 9th. I had just spent three days walking round the vast estuary of the Solway Firth, always seeing Scotland over the other side, but knowing I would have to walk all the way to Carlisle before I would reach a bridge over the river. Many years ago there was a train along the south bank of the Solway Firth all the way to Bowness-on-Solway, with a rail tunnel under the Solway itself to Annan, in Scotland. I was told that children from this area of Cumbria had gone to school in Scotland using this route. Now, however, there was no way across except via the bridge at Carlisle.

For most of the time the Solway Firth was a vast expanse of sand—rather like another Morecambe Bay. Indeed, like Morecambe Bay, the Solway is notorious for its quicksands, and its tide comes in even more swiftly than at Morecambe Bay—being the fastest incoming tide in the world.

At length I reached "The First House in Scotland" at Gretna. I got myself photographed next to it in true tourist fashion, and then set off, now walking along the north bank of the Solway. By that night I had reached the village of Eastriggs, near Annan, where I'd planned to camp as I knew the village had a campsite. However, since it was pouring with rain when I arrived I decided to stay under cover, and I started looking for a "B & B" sign.

The Scots' legendary reputation for meanness is thoroughly undeserved; in fact, completely untrue. They were the most hospitable people in the whole country; they helped me out, gave me meals, put me up in their homes for the night. But, perhaps not surprisingly, many of them are rather sensitive about their undeserved reputation, and this can cause them to bend over backwards to show that it isn't true. This fact I was about to discover.

The house in Eastriggs where I enquired about overnight accommodation did have vacancies, and I was shown to a most pleasant room and offered a cup of tea, which I gratefully accepted. Five minutes later a large pot of tea appeared, accompanied by a plate of scones, oatcakes, and biscuits. It looked like enough for about four people, and my surprise must have shown on my face, for my hostess laughed.

"I'm sure you need a wee snack after walking in this rain, lassie," she said. "Anyway, I wanted to show you the Scots aren't mean."

Now I had lived for five years in Edinburgh when I was a student, and I quickly assured her I was familiar with Scotland and I knew the Scots weren't mean. But I'm not at all sure that this registered. For an hour later I had my nose happily buried in a book, having decided to spend the evening reading and resting, when there was a knock on my door.

"What are you doing for your supper, lassie?" enquired my hostess.

I was fairly used to this sort of question. Often I would fix myself an instant packet soup along with a sandwich in the evening if I was staying at bed and breakfast accommodation and therefore getting a huge traditional breakfast, unless I really wanted to go out for a meal. I had found I didn't actually need all that much food, and this worked well and was all I wanted. But I often had a hard time convincing other people that I was getting enough to eat, for many of them were sure that since I was walking so much I must need enormous quantities of food. This attitude was so prevalent that many guest house proprietors had to be almost forcibly prevented from cooking me a large meal I neither needed nor wanted.

However, this wasn't what my Scottish hostess had in mind.

"Me and Morag here," she said, indicating the comfortable-looking grey-haired woman she had previously introduced as her cousin. "Me and Morag, we're going to have a wee snack. So I made one for you too."

69

I protested that it really wasn't necessary. I wasn't at all hungry, for I was still feeling full from my earlier "wee snack".

"Oh, but you must eat," said my hostess, in a tone which brooked no argument. "And don't worry, I won't charge you for it. We wouldn't want you to think the Scots were mean."

I could see that she was quite determined, so I gave up and followed her downstairs. The "wee snack" turned out to be two rounds of generously-filled sandwiches, more oatcakes, and another large pot of tea. It was quite delicious and I didn't want to appear ungrateful. But now I really was absolutely full.

Two hours later, as I began to think about having an early night, there was another knock on my door.

"Well, are you coming down for your tea?" The broad Scots voice sounded mildly exasperated, like I was a wayward child who was late, again.

I listened in utter disbelief. Hospitality was one thing, but this was becoming ridiculous. Besides, did they think I had a bottomless pit in place of a stomach? I nearly told my hostess I wasn't coming, but I didn't want to offend her. Besides, I told myself, I could probably manage to drink just one cup of tea.

So I dutifully went downstairs again, but as I entered the sitting room I stopped, almost aghast by this point. There, by the side of the fire, was yet another tray piled high with oatcakes and biscuits, plus another large pot of tea—in other words, another Scottish "wee snack".

Next morning I had the usual huge "B & B type" breakfast—cereal, fry-up, toast with marmalade, and tea. In addition there were a few typical Scottish extras such as oatcakes and honey. I reflected that if this place was typical of Scottish bed and breakfast establishments I'd weigh twenty stone by the time I got back to England. I also began to wonder how the proprietors of such places made any money—the rates here had been reasonable by anyone's standards.

At length I left Eastriggs—feeling somewhat bloated—with good wishes ringing in my ears and more assurances that the Scots really weren't mean. I believed it.

I rapidly discovered that this experience, as far as Scottish bed and breakfast places were concerned, had been fairly typical. And it wasn't just the bed and breakfast proprietors who were so over-whelmingly generous; it was nearly everyone. When I reached Newton Stewart the warden of the nearby youth hostel allowed me to stay at no charge, in exchange for what was really a token amount of help in the hostel. He was extremely helpful, making sure I had a good rest, and finding maps and route information for my next few days walking. Then in Lendalfoot, on the Ayrshire coast almost op-posite the Isle of Arran, I stopped to chat to a family who were sitting in the sun outside their holiday cottage. On hearing what I was doing, they instantly invited me to stay overnight in their caravan and join them for a meal. A few days later, I walked past a caravan which was parked by the side of the road for the night. The people in it were having breakfast, and they immediately invited me to join them. And several weeks after this I found myself camp-ing on a rainy night in an isolated area, the campsite being the only possible place to stay for several miles. It looked like being a depressing evening, until I met a Glaswegian family in the campsite restaurant, who insisted I go back to their large, luxurious caravan for a shower, meal, and game of cards. It really was quite astonishing, and it became clear to me that it's the Scots' hospitality which should be legendary, not their meanness.

My 'hooped bivi' tent

Towards the end of July I reached Ayr, where Miriam and Yudi met me for the third and last time, until I reached Brighton many months later. It was becoming just too expensive and time-consuming to meet me now I was so far away, Miriam explained. I found myself a bit mystified by this. My brain couldn't grasp that it could be expensive to get from the South-East of England to the west coast of Scotland since, after all, I had walked there. Walking round Britain gives you a strange perspective on things like that.

Ayr was memorable in a number of small ways. Firstly, I acquired my only blister of the walk. It may seem hard to believe, but I'd had no trouble at all with blisters at the start. I think this is because I'd scrupulously rubbed my feet with surgical spirit for a month before I set out, and my boots had been well broken in and comfortable. But I hadn't been able to break in the new boots I'd picked up in Carlisle, so now, after all this time, I had a blister. I was really rather annoyed.

In Ayr I also acquired what was to be one of my favourite possessions for the duration of the walk. I was with Miriam and Yudi in a market, when we saw a stall which sold teeshirts with one's name on them, mainly for children of course. Now the day before I'd confessed to Yudi, half-jokingly, that I fancied a teeshirt with "I'm walking round Britain" on it. So when she saw this stall, she instantly dragged me over.

"Can you do a teeshirt with 'I'm walking round Britain' on it," she asked, before I could protest that I hadn't really meant it. They could, and did. And although I felt like something of a show-off wearing it, I actually loved it. It made a good talking point in pubs and cafes, and provided an opportunity for new comments, which made a welcome change from the constant "That's a big pack you've got there", which was beginning after all this time to get on my nerves.

So after a good day's rest in Ayr with my friends I was off again, continuing up the coast. I walked to Ardrossan, and here took the ferry over to the Isle of Arran. This was the beginning of my longest "short cut" of the trip.

My reasons for going to Arran were essentially practical. Scotland is much larger than most people realise, or than I had realised, anyway. From Gretna Green to the north coast is about four hundred miles; even at Inverness one is still over a hundred miles from John o'Groats. In addition it has an enormous amount of coastline; in fact, nearly as much as the whole of England and Wales together. This is mainly because of the large number of inlets, sea lochs and peninsulas on the west coast; indeed, I often felt as though one could spend a lifetime just walking round the west coast of Scotland.

Before I'd started the walk I hadn't really worried about timing. Along with the rest of my non-planning, I'd figured I could sort something out. After all, I'd reasoned, I might never get past Lands End, so it was silly to worry about how I'd survive a winter in Scotland. But when I reached the Scottish border on July 9th I realised it was necessary to take stock of my situation. For walking through northern Scotland in winter just wasn't a practical proposition—the weather could be appalling, the hours of daylight were very short, and most camp sites and other places offering accommodation were closed. So I decided that to be realistic I would have to have some deadlines, and I made up my mind that if I was to walk round Scotland at all I would have to reach Cape Wrath, the North-West corner, by the end of August. This would make it possible to cross back into England by the end of October. I would have to plan my route accordingly, taking short cuts where necessary and using the concept of "coast" rather more flexibly than I had so far.

There are numerous ways of doing this; indeed, most people who have walked or cycled round Britain have ended up taking quite drastic short cuts in Scotland. Some have stuck to the roads, since footpaths in isolated areas of Scotland are virtually non-existent anyway; this effectively reduces the distance by hundreds of miles. Others have called everything south of the Crinan Canal an island; this, in one stroke, cuts out the long peninsula of Kintyre and a relatively large area north of it.

However, I didn't want to do either of these, since to do so would mean missing out some of the most beautiful coastal scenery in the world. So I came up with my own route; a route which was, as far as I knew, unique in the history of British coastal walking. I was fairly certain it had never been walked before in the exact form in which I did it. I decided to treat the Firth of Clyde, which extends all the way from the Ayrshire coast up to Glasgow and back down to the Mull of Kintyre, as a large river. The Isle of Arran, I decided, was a stepping stone in the middle of this river. Therefore I would take a ferry to Arran, and another from there to Kintyre. From Claonaig, on Kintyre, I would follow the coast reasonably closely round the Mull of Kintyre and up to Oban; then, similarly, I would use the Isle of Mull as a short cut to reach the Ardnmurchan peninsula. I would carry on up to Mallaig, from where I could get a boat to the Isle of Skye. This would save the time which would otherwise be involved in negotiating the wild, trackless, and heavily indented stretch of mainland north of Mallaig. Once having crossed back to Kyle of Lochalsh, I could then fairly easily follow the coast all the way to Cape Wrath. I estimated that by this means I could reach the north coast by the end of August without too much difficulty, but if this proved to be over-optimistic or I got held up, I would take further short cuts in similar fashion.

This plan worked out surprisingly well. The main difficulty—in fact, the only one—arose because of people's reactions to it. For a start, the inhabitants of Arran didn't like their island being called a stepping stone. I'm not at all certain why not—I had no intention of being insulting—but for some reason it bothered them. So on Arran I found myself compelled to keep quiet about my reasons for this route, and this meant I didn't say much about the walk in general. Still, this could hardly be classed as a real problem.

Then there were the self-styled walking purists. I really can't understand why people who'd never even dream of walking round Britain themselves should have the presumption to tell those who do exactly how it should be done. But they do, and my route infuriated this type of person.

"You're not walking round the coast," I would be told, many times, by one of these people.

"OK, OK," I'd respond placatingly. "That's fine; so I'm just walking round Britain, by whatever route I feel like."

"You're not even doing that," the person would continue in angry disgust. "You're getting boats. I mean, where do you draw the line? Someone could get a boat right round the whole country and say they were walking round Britain."

"Does it matter?" I would think, a trifle wearily. For I never understood this attitude. People could do or say anything they liked as far as I was concerned; it wasn't my problem. Since I wasn't trying to set a record, and I wasn't raising money for charity under false pretences, what did it matter what I did, or what I called it? Anyway, as far as I could see it only concerned me; it was nobody else's business.

Soon after my crossing to Arran I ran into someone I had been hoping to meet for months. I had crossed from Arran to Kintyre, then walked to a small resort called Carradale. I had just erected my tent on the campsite there, when I saw what was, for a family holiday resort like Carradale, an unusual sight. Standing by the camp shop was a man in perhaps his later fifties, grey-haired and bearded, with hiking boots and a backpack even larger than my own.

The germ of a suspicion entered my mind. I knew that at about the time I started to walk round the coast, someone else had set off to do the same thing, but going in the opposite direction. I had heard that this man, Ron Bullen, was about twenty years older than I was, and very fit. Was this Ron Bullen, I wondered? This man easily could be; he was about the right age, and looked like a serious walker. I would find out.

As I approached, I heard the man describing to an interested bystander how he had been lost in fog on the Mull of Kintyre earlier that day. It must be Ron Bullen. Who but a round Britain walker would even try to walk round the Mull of Kintyre in the appalling weather we'd had recently? As I waited for a lull in the conversation, the bystander turned an indulgent smile on me.

"I think she's absolutely fascinated by you," he said to the walker, giving him a knowing wink.

This infuriated me. What did he think I was—some kind of walking groupie? However, knowing the circumstances, I smiled brightly at him.

"Actually," I said calmly, "I think I'm doing exactly the same thing he is, and that's why I want to meet him."

I turned to the walker. "I'm Helen Krasner," I told him. "I'm walking round the coast of Britain. Are you Ron Bullen by any chance?"

He was, he had heard of me, and he was delighted to meet me. The bystander found himself totally ignored. It served him right.

Ron and I then commenced to have a conversation which clearly illustrated the fact that we were poles apart in terms of our attitudes to walking.

"Yes, it's going well," he told me in reply to my query about his walk. "I'm up on schedule now, but I was two days behind a while back. But it's a bitch of a walk, a real bitch!"

He sounded nervous, tired, and like a man under a lot of stress.

"Still," he continued, "I'll get the record, and that's what counts. I'll be doing 7,003 miles, and that's more than John Merrill did. And I'll finish in nine months too, if I don't fall behind schedule again. And I'll be the oldest person to do it."

He shuffled a bit, obviously in some pain.

"My feet are giving me real trouble though," he confided. "I've chipped some of the bones. A doctor told me to stop walking, but I can't do that. I'll have to keep going; I can ignore the pain if I have to."

He didn't sound as though he was enjoying the walk at all. His talk was totally alien to me; all of records and mileages. What about the countryside, I wondered? And the people and wildlife and local customs—all the hundreds of things which made the walk so memorable for me? Didn't he even see these things? Was he completely oblivious to everything except finishing the walk and breaking a record?

At last Ron turned to me.

"Going for the women s record, are you?" he enquired.

The way he said it made it a statement, rather than a question—he apparently felt the answer was obvious.

"What women's record?" I asked, genuinely surprised. He stared at me, obviously dumbfounded. I don't think he knew what to say. Neither did I, for it was becoming clear to me that we might both be walking round Britain, but we barely spoke the same language.

The rest of the conversation proved this to be the case. Ron recovered himself and congratulated me on my great achievement. I just stopped myself from asking, "What achievement?" He told me the Mull of Kintyre was "a bitch". I shrugged and said in that case I'd skip it altogether, which clearly horrified him. I told him how much I'd liked Arran, talking animatedly of the day I'd spent lying in the sun enjoying a short heatwave, and sightseeing. He said nothing to this, but it was quite clearly something he'd never even consider doing while on the walk—for him rest days were absolutely taboo.

By the time we parted I think we had perhaps developed a mutual respect, but nothing more. I certainly couldn't help but admire Ron's dedication—but I didn't understand him at all. I think his feelings about me were probably somewhat similar.

Next day I left Carradale and continued walking—my way. By now I was reasonably experienced, fairly fit, and thoroughly enjoying the walk. That evening I reached Campbeltown, the largest town on Kintyre, and here I decided to do something I should have done about three months earlier; namely, visit a doctor. For actually Ron Bullen wasn't the only person having trouble with his feet. In spite of the fact I felt really fit and well, my right foot had actually been hurting for several months. There was a steady ache on the top of it which bothered me quite a lot at the end of the day. However, if I laced my boots tightly enough it wasn't really a problem, and so I had ignored it for a long time.

"Far too long," the nurse I met on Arran had told me. We had been chatting and I'd asked her casually what I could do about my foot. When I'd described the symptoms she had shaken her head disapprovingly.

"It sound like maybe you've cracked the bone," she had said. "It might be a stress fracture. You should see a doctor."

"But they'll try to stop me walking," I had protested. Since I wasn't in really bad pain I found it hard to believe there could be anything seriously wrong, and I don't like going to the doctor at the best of times.

The nurse looked at me as though I was a stupid child.

"No, they won't," she explained patiently. "They'll just strap up your foot so you can walk on it without any pain or further damage."

I'd had to admit this sounded like common sense. So, since Campbeltown was the last place with a hospital for many miles— probably until Oban—when I arrived there I duly presented myself at the morning out-patients clinic.

I must have looked rather out of place in the cottage hospital in this small, remote Scottish town. Since I was planning to continue walking that day—unless there really was something seriously wrong with my foot—I was wearing all my walking gear and carrying my backpack. The waiting room was crowded, and there was nowhere to put my pack. I had to apologise to an old man who nearly fell over it, then try to make room for a harassed mother with three children in tow. By this time I think the locals were wondering what on earth I was doing there, and in fact I was wondering myself.

At last it was my turn to see the doctor, and I explained about my foot. He listened carefully; he was a middle-aged, comfortable-looking country doctor, a man who looked as though he rarely walked if he could drive. I suspect he thought my pack and boots were a bit of an affectation.

"Have you been doing any unaccustomed walking?" he asked when I had finished. It sounded like a routine question, the type of thing he asked anyone who complained of an aching foot.

"Well," I said, "I've been walking about twenty miles a day for the last five months."

I said it casually, as though it was the most normal thing in the world. For me it was, but actually I was feeling rather bored and enjoyed anticipating the effect my words might have.

In this respect I wasn't disappointed. I'm not sure if the doctor's jaw actually dropped, but he was certainly rendered speechless. He gazed at me in blank amazement, his expression saying more plainly than any words could that he wasn't in the least surprised my foot hurt. He'd probably have been more surprised if it didn't.

Nevertheless, after yanking my toes and pummelling my heel in what seems to be traditional medical fashion, the doctor suggested I have the foot X-rayed.

"I don't think you've broken anything," he told me, his composure now somewhat returned. "I think it's just that you aren't giving your foot a chance to rest. But we'd better be sure."

The X-ray duly showed—to my relief—a set of unbroken bones, and I began to get ready to set off again. However, the doctor wasn't finished yet.

"Phone us next Saturday," he told me. "I'd like to check that X-ray with the experts."

I promised to do so, and again began to prepare to leave, but the doctor had still further plans.

"Go and see the physiotherapist now," he continued. "Maybe she can give you some exercises for your foot."

This sounded crazy, since exercise was the cause of the trouble, and I said as much. However, the doctor explained that specific exercises to strengthen the arch might be what I needed.

"We'll see if we can t do something for you," he said, "Since the foot still hurts."

Then he grinned, and looked almost young.

"And since I can see you're not prepared to stop walking if you don't absolutely have to," he told me as a parting shot.

A perceptive man, that doctor.

It was midday before I managed to leave Campbeltown. The nurse gave me bandages and foam pads for my foot, and the physiotherapist taught me a variety of arch-strengthening exercises. The radiographer reminded me to phone the following week about the X-ray, and they all gave me their good wishes before I left. I suppose it wasn't every day they had a round Britain walker with a suspected stress fracture, so I think I was a bit of an event for Campbeltown.

By the following Saturday, when the time came to phone the hospital about the X-ray, I was on the Ardnamurchan peninsula in the Highlands. This is one of the most desolate areas in the whole country, and I knew I was unlikely to find a telephone after I left the village of Kilchoan. My foot had been improving all week; the bandages and exercises were definitely a help. Still, I decided I'd better phone the hospital and check the verdict of the "experts" on my X-ray. The only problem was that Kilchoan was quite deserted and I only had one ten-pence piece for the phone. That should be enough though, I thought. I only needed the answer to one question.

I was lucky; I got through to the radiographer immediately.

"Of course I remember you," she said in response to my rather garbled explanation of who I was. "How are you getting on?"

"Fine," I responded, "Can you tell …"

"And how's the weather up there?" interrupted the radiographer. "It's been better down here recently."

"It's nice here too," I replied, getting a bit tense and hoping she'd finish soon, before we got cut off. "Can you tell me …"

"Your walk sounded fascinating," continued the radiographer. "Where are you now?"

"Kilchoan," I gasped, acutely conscious now of the ever-decreasing number of telephone units and the fact I had no change left at all. "Please can you tell me …"

"Where's Kilchoan?" asked the radiographer brightly, obviously in the mood for a friendly chat and quite oblivious to my predicament. I began to get desperate.

"The X-ray!" I blurted out, almost yelling, expecting to be cut off at any moment. "Can you tell me…"

"Oh, yes, your foot," said the radiographer calmly. "Don't worry, it's fine. There's nothing broken at all."

She had told me in the nick of time. The pips went, and we were cut off.

From Campbeltown I crossed the peninsula of Kintyre, passing close to Paul MacCartney's farm. I had threatened to knock on his door and introduce myself, but I never managed to find out exactly where he lived. I continued north, through some of the least-known but most beautiful countryside in Britain, sometimes camping, occasionally finding bed and breakfast accommodation. Finally, on August 4th, I reached the bustling town of Oban, gateway to the Highlands and Islands.

Chapter 7

The Highlands

Oban in mid-summer is busy and crowded. From here thousands of people catch boats to the islands and trains to the far north; the town really lives up to its title of Gateway to the Highlands and Islands. It is also full of backpackers, and in Oban nobody as much as glanced at my large backpack, which was quite a relief. I fitted in perfectly; I looked just like everybody else.

I spent a day in Oban sightseeing and stocking up on supplies, since it was the only large town I expected to see for quite a while. Then I caught a boat to the Isle of Mull. This was another of my short cuts, for from here I would catch another ferry to the Ardnamurchan peninsula, westernmost point of Britain. From the ferry landing I walked along the coast of Mull until I reached Tobermory, the main town and a famous sailing centre.

I was to pick up mail at the youth hostel in Tobermory, the first time I had received any for several weeks. My arrangements for mail were complicated but quite well organised. Everything was sent to my parents' address, and I phoned my mother at frequent intervals to tell her where to forward it, after I had arranged a suitable pick-up point. In this instance I had telephoned the warden of Tobermory youth hostel several weeks earlier to ask if she could keep mail for me. She had warned me that her hostel was small and very short of space in mid-summer; however, she had agreed to keep my mail so long as there wouldn't be too much of it. I had no reason to expect a large amount—I hadn't received many letters since I'd left Brighton—so there seemed to be no problem.

But things had changed. I should have been forewarned of this a week earlier, when I had phoned my mother for a chat.

"I think you need a full-time secretary," she had announced, sounding only half-joking.

I asked her what she meant.

"Well," she continued, "I've forwarded twenty-three letters this week, and seventeen last. My hand's getting tired. What's going on?"

I didn't know, and the significance of what she was saying didn't hit me at the time. However, when I reached Tobermory youth hostel I found out. The warden glared at me reproachfully, then silently handed me an absolutely huge box of mail. It had, she told me, been taking up a lot of much-needed space in her tiny office. Could I please get things sent to larger hostels in future. She wasn't a post office.

Muttering profuse apologies, I took the box up to my room. What were all these letters, I wondered? How come I suddenly had so much mail?

When I had opened them I was amazed. For in the box were over fifty letters, from people living all round the coast of Britain, all of them offering me a place to stay when I reached their area. It was just what I needed, and it solved my accommodation and financial problems at one stroke. It also provided me with a first-rate opportunity to meet people.

How had this happened? Well, about three months into the walk I had had the idea of writing to both the YHA Magazine and one of the specialist walking magazines, telling them what I was doing. Would any of their readers, I had asked, be able to put me up for a night when I passed through their areas? Could they ask, through the pages of their respective magazines?

I had then completely forgotten about it. But both magazines had printed my request, and both articles had appeared within a week of each other. The response had been tremendous, better than I could ever have imagined, and this accounted for the sudden deluge of mail. Some people appeared, in their enthusiasm, to have misunderstood—an offer of accommodation in Birmingham, however well-meant, really wasn't much use on a coastal walk. All the same, I had over forty replies from people in places I would be walking through, and this would be very useful indeed.

This was only one example of the growing changes in attitude towards me as the walk progressed. I had noticed this occurring gradually as I went around the coast. Near the start, when I told people what I was doing, they were amused. By the time I reached Wales the usual response was astonishment. But from Northern England onwards it was rapidly turning to admiration. People no longer asked me if I thought I'd make it. I had walked nearly 2,000 miles; I was fit and healthy; I was making it. They could see it.

The publicity I started to receive from local media now began to produce other responses too. I received donations of maps and route planning information through the post from all kinds of sources. People who worked on local radio stations or newspapers wrote to me asking if I could contact them when I passed through their area. Several people wrote asking for advice on long distance walking. Others just asked if they could meet me, or talk to me. I was even sent a donation of money "towards your next pair of boots". And other long distance walkers wanted to meet me; I was contacted by a man who'd walked round the whole of Scotland, and by two of the first people to climb all of Scotland's 3,000 foot mountains. I also made plans to meet Vera Andrews, the only other woman—so far as anyone knew—to have walked round Britain, when I passed by her home in Clacton-on-Sea.

Suddenly I was beginning to be considered a celebrity, and an expert. Nobody seemed to have any further doubts as to whether or not I'd complete the walk. Nobody except me, that is, and I didn't have time to dwell on it. For I had to organise the next stretch of walking—round the desolate Ardnamurchan peninsula.

"The north coast of where?" asked the woman in the tourist office in Tobermory, in reply to my query. "Which coast of Ardnamurchan?"

I sighed inwardly. Her reaction was typical of the responses I was meeting to my questions about the feasibility of walking round the

Ardnamurchan peninsula. I just wanted to know if it was possible to walk round this beautiful but wild-looking region which I could see just across the Sound of Mull. Did the footpaths marked on the map exist? How much difficulty was I likely to have if I attempted this walk? They seemed to be fairly routine questions in an area popular with walkers, yet I was meeting with complete and utter ignorance. It appeared as though nobody had ever been to the north coast of Ardnamurchan.

So difficult was it to obtain information that I had almost decided to give up the idea. I made up my mind to simply follow the roads. And I would probably have done this but for one thing. The day I caught the ferry from Tobermory to Ardnamurchan was warm and sunny, a complete contrast to the inhospitable weather of the previous few days. It was actually, though I didn't then know it, the start of a week-long heatwave in the Highlands. I'd noticed before that my sense of adventure and inclination to take risks increased in direct proportion to the number of hours of sunshine, and this time was no exception. I decided that I really wanted to walk that north coast. So I would do it, somehow.

On leaving the boat I set out for the village of Kilchoan. Here I found a small shop and stocked up on food and other supplies. It was the last shop I was to see for over two days.

From the village I followed the road to the Point of Ardnamurchan. This was the "main" road—in fact the only one along that coast. However, it was single-track and rarely used, being more or less a well-paved footpath. This was the case with many roads in the north-west Highlands. For now I was in the far north, Britain's only wilderness area.

I reached the Point of Ardnamurchan about midday. It was August 9th, the height of the holiday season, and only two days before the queen's well-publicised visit to the region. Ardnamurchan Point is the most westerly point of Britain, the true "lands end". But the most notable thing about it was the complete absence of other people; there was nobody there at all. I couldn't help but compare it to my arrival at the other Lands End, the wellknown one, in Cornwall. There, on a cold, blustery day in early spring, there had been crowds. But here, on a beautiful afternoon in mid-summer, I ate my sandwiches below the lighthouse, looking out over the deep blue expanse of the sea, with only the gulls for company.

This was typical of the Highlands, I discovered. It is the one area of Britain which you can visit in July or August and still have space to breathe, in fact have it virtually to yourself. There are vast tracts of the most beautiful countryside, with some of the best scenery and beaches in the world, which are visited by nobody except the most adventurous travellers. Here you can walk for miles without seeing a soul, share golden beaches with only the birds and seals, and swim in the sea—surprisingly warm due to the gulf stream's influence—without fighting your way through children or sailboards. It's hardly surprising that I fell in love with the far north.

The locals told me later that there is a path starting from the Ardnamurchan lighthouse and going along the north coast. However, I never managed to find it, for footpath signposts are something the Highlands doesn't seem to have heard of yet. So I ended up following the road—another single-track affair—around to the village of Sanna, a tiny resort with a deservedly famous sandy beach. Famous, that is, among the relatively few people who actually know about it. From this point on, there appeared to be no path at all, according to the map, for the next two or three miles. I wasn't sure what to do, and decided to see if any of the people in the area knew anything about it.

At this point I ran into John and Sue, a couple who were holidaying in the area, and had a leaflet describing local walks. This leaflet stated that from three miles further along there was a well-defined footpath all round the rest of the north coast—a good two days walking. This was wonderful, but what was I to do for the first three miles? John's leaflet described this as "an interesting, though trackless route". I knew from much recent experience that this should be translated as "a rough scramble better suited to mountain goats." But the sun was still shining, so I still felt reasonably adventurous. What finally decided me was the fact that John and Sue decided they would accompany me on the first stretch, if I would like them to.

"It'll be a nice walk," declared John. "Only three miles; it won't take long."

It would be nice to have company, I thought, and I readily agreed.

John was wrong. The three miles turned out to be at least five, by the time we'd lost our way several times and negotiated the bogs, fences, streams and other obstacles in our path. And it felt like at least ten. In fact, after about an hour John and Sue gave up. It was getting too late, they explained, and their feet were soaked; they were sorry, but they really had to go back. They hoped I would be alright; I had to reach the path soon.

I continued on. Yes, I had to reach the path soon—but where was it? It was getting late, and I was beginning to get worried. I was even wondering if I had somehow managed to miss the path altogether, although this would be nearly impossible as it ran—according to the map—at right angles to my "trackless route". I was about to panic when I slipped and literally stumbled over the path. I heaved a sigh of relief. Now I could relax.

I camped that night in an idyllic little glade by a stream, with views right over the sea to the islands beyond. The local farmer whose permission I'd asked had looked at me in surprise.

"You can camp wherever you like," he told me. "People just camp anywhere." This was said with an expansive gesture across the hills, obviously implying that there was plenty of room for all of us. It was good to be somewhere where this was so—nowhere in Britain but the Highlands would it be possible.

The next morning another single-track road led to the only village on the north Ardnamurchan coast; it had about half a dozen houses and a post office consisting of a tiny shed with hens scratching in the back yard. I knocked on the post office door, hoping they might perhaps sell food or bars of chocolate, as so many isolated post offices do. It would be nice to supplement my monotonous camping diet of the past couple of days. They didn't sell any food, but the postmistress invited me in for a cup of tea and a snack, giving me all she could find and even apologising for her slightly stale rolls and the lack of any cakes. It was my first taste of Highland hospitality, though by no means my last.

From here I continued along a well-defined path, through what must be some of the most breathtakingly beautiful scenery in the world. And I was by now something of an expert. In fact, throughout the walk I had had a kind of unofficial contest in my mind for the most beautiful section of coastline. Before this I think South Cornwall, Pembrokeshire, and the Isle of Arran had all been about neck and neck. But the north coast of Ardnamurchan beat them all; it was most definitely my prize winner. Its broken, heavily indented coastline, with stupendous views over to the islands of Rhum, Eigg and Muck, is quite out of this world. I spent much of the day just sitting in the sunshine, staring at the views, and again marvelling at the fact that I had it all to myself. For in spite of the fact that it was now a weekend, in August, I didn't see a soul all day. Nothing but two adventurous sheep.

I finally reached the main road. I camped the next night at a lovely campsite by a huge loch, and continued north up the coast the following day.

That night came the first hitch in what had been an idyllic few days. I found a place to camp beside a small stream, not far from the road. It looked quite suitable, but what I didn't notice was that I was in long grass on very low lying ground. And I didn't realise that these conditions amounted to invitations to Scotland's most ferocious beast, the midge.

Scottish midges are justly notorious. I had heard that from June to about October they swarm in their thousands, making life utterly miserable for anyone caught outside after dark. People had told me that they created utter havoc, even being reputed to have driven people stark staring mad in some instances. I heard amazing tales of people being driven from their beds and running wildly into the night to escape a horde of midges. Many people actually left their homes in the midge season, and one Scotsman, driven to illogical fury by these tiny torturers, complained to me:

"I wouldn't mind if they just attacked the sassenachs. But they go for the locals too."

I had of course encountered Scottish midges before, for the midge season had been well under way for some weeks. But I felt that the stories were grossly exaggerated. That is, until this particular night. For on account of the warm weather and the spot I had picked to camp, they swarmed in their thousands, and within a few minutes it dawned on me that I couldn't possibly ignore them and there was no way of escape. So I did the only thing possible—I dived in my tent, closed the mosquito net, and stayed there. I could see the little monsters hovering outside, lying in wait. Well, they weren't going to get me. I wouldn't come out till morning.

But I had forgotten one thing. I groaned aloud in sudden despair as I realised I just had to have a pee. I tried to ignore it, but it was no use; I would have to go out. I pulled on all my clothes—woolly hat, long-sleeved shirt, socks—anything to protect me from the waiting midges. Then, heart in my mouth, I ventured out. Surely, I thought hopefully, surely I couldn't get bitten by that many midges in such a short time.

It was now just about dusk, and there must have been literally millions of them. In no time at all they covered my clothes and got in my hair; then as I breathed in they got up my nose and in my mouth. Soon I was black from head to foot—it was like some kind of bizarre horror film. I could really understand now how people went mad; for I had to keep a firm grip on things in order not to run screaming into the night myself. As soon as I possibly could I dived back into the tent. I had no intention of coming out again until morning for any reason whatsoever; supper, teeth-cleaning, and all the other trappings of civilisation would have to wait.

The next day the sun shone, the midges were forgotten, and I reached Garramore youth hostel, near the Isle of Skye. The following day was my birthday, and yet another hot sunny day. I spent the day lying on a magnificent deserted beach of silver sand, improving my suntan as I gazed across at Skye in the distance. Why, I wondered drowsily, does anyone leave Britain for holidays?

But the next day I remembered why, when I woke up to pouring rain. I packed my gear, walked the five miles to Mallaig, and caught the boat to Skye, my final island short cut. Since it was still raining I took refuge for the rest of the day in a guest house, and the next day continued on and crossed back to the mainland. I was feeling good, for it was still only the middle of August, and I had walked almost the whole west coast. I was well up on the schedule I had been forced to make, and if things continued smoothly I would soon be at Cape Wrath, and so be well south before winter arrived.

From Kyle of Lochalsh, on the mainland just across from Skye, I walked to Plockton, where I camped for the night. This picturesque village is warmed by a branch of the gulf stream, so that in spite of its extreme northerly location it has palm trees lining its main street. It thus has something of a Mediterranean feel to it, and it was hard to believe I was in northern Scotland. My camera clicked incessantly as I photographed the main street from every angle; Miriam had wanted me to send her photos of palm trees in Torquay—I would go one better and send palm trees in Plockton.

From here I followed the coast to Lochcarron and Kishorn. From Kishorn the actual coast was impassable now, though in the last century there was a "coffin path"—a route by which the dead were carried from isolated villages. However, this path is long since overgrown, so I went by road, climbing the 2,000 foot high "Pass of the Cattle" to Applecross. This road, one of the highest in Britain, winds up the steep valley sides to the desolate and dramatic pass at the top. The road is narrow and dangerous, and has a sign at its entrance stating that it is unsuitable for learner drivers or large vehicles. The sign didn't say anything about coast path walkers, but it took all my experience and endurance to manage the last mile of the six mile steep climb to the top. The view, however, made it all worth it, as did the curious young deer I met near the summit, friendly and quite unafraid. I think she was fascinated by seeing a human being on foot, as she'd probably only seen them in cars before she met me.

Palm trees in Plockton

I was now in one of the most wild and uninhabited areas of Britain, where one could travel for miles without coming across a village, and each house could be a few miles from its neighbour. In this region I was forced to carry three or four days supply of food, for I never knew when I might possibly reach a shop or restaurant. In many ways travelling up here is even harder for people touring by car, for garages are exceedingly few and far between. Most people who have toured the far north have a story to tell of the time they almost ran out of petrol on a lonely mountain road. And those who ran out on a Sunday had an even harder time. For here the Scottish Free Church rules, and Sunday is a day of rest, absolutely.

My first experience of a Sunday in the far north occurred the day I left Applecross to follow the "new road", built in 1979, round the whole of the Applecross peninsula. This led me through a sparsely populated area, with scattered farmhouses and tiny villages at intervals along the route. It was a sight common in the far north, but on the day I walked through this region things looked very strange. There wasn't a soul in sight; tractors lay abandoned in the fields; sheep and cows wandered at will. Farming is normally an occupation for seven days of the week, and I had never before been in a farming area where there wasn't some sign of activity, whatever the day. Not knowing much about the Highland Sabbath at the time, I began to wonder, a shade fancifully I must admit, whether some disaster had struck or the Martians had landed. Where was everybody?

That evening I reached the small village of Kenmore, where according to my guidebook there was a family who provided bed and breakfast. Since it was now raining, I knocked hopefully at their door, but they told me apologetically that they were full. However, they agreed to my request to sleep in their barn, since the weather was really too bad for camping. I was surprised they were full in such an isolated area, but I wouldn't normally have thought any more about it. But one thing seemed very strange—I was there all evening, yet not one person came or went from this "full" bed and breakfast establishment.

Late in the evening I discovered the probable explanation. The farmer dropped in to check I had all I needed, and during our ensuing conversation he invited me to go over to the house for a shower the next morning. At that carefully emphasised "next morning", the penny dropped. Of course; it was Sunday. They weren't willing to have anyone staying overnight, but hadn't wanted to be completely inhospitable to a stranger. I had put them into quite a predicament by asking to stay, so they had compromised by letting me use their barn and offering me a shower—but on Monday.

I heard a story along somewhat similar lines from a woman who had lived for many years in a small village further north, close to Lochinver. Edna and her husband Andrew had only recently arrived when Andrew had to go away on business for a weekend. Edna had needed to phone him on the Sunday to make arrangements for his return home, but her phone was out of order. So she had gone to ask some neighbours if she could use their phone, and had been most confused by their reaction.

"Oh," the woman of the house had said, obviously uncomfortable, clearly not knowing what to do. "Alright. Come in. The phone's there." She had gestured vaguely, almost as though she was trying to pretend she wasn't doing it.

So Edna had made her phone call, while wondering what was wrong. For the couple—her friends—had stood there watching her, obviously ill at ease. They quite clearly didn't like her being there, which was most uncharacteristic of them. She couldn't think what was going on. Her phone call completed, she had tried to chat, to make friendly small talk, but to no avail. Without being rude, her neighbours had made it perfectly clear she wasn't wanted.

The next day she was even more puzzled, for her neighbour had welcomed her warmly, in absolute contrast to her behaviour the previous day:

"Come in Edna; how are you? And how was Andrew when you phoned? When will he be coming back? You must be getting lonely on your own. Do let us know if you need anything."

The neighbour had continued chatting, bustling around, making tea, acting quite normally. She had offered no explanation for her attitude the day before and it was some time before Edna had realised you just didn't ask to use a Highlander's phone on the Sabbath. This had been the whole problem.

Perhaps the most enviable quality about the Highlanders, it seemed to me, was their capacity for enjoyment. In this far-flung region, winters are long and organised forms of leisure few, yet the people I met were adept at creating their own entertainment and organising rapidly in almost any circumstances. I heard of a wedding reception which was arranged at twenty-four hours notice in the local hotel in a tiny village; they spread the news by word of mouth, and ended up with 200 people from the whole surrounding area—a resounding success by any standards. And I couldn't help but laugh at a story I overheard at a pub where I stopped for lunch one day, in another small village. The landlady was describing how, for about the first time in living memory, the police had appeared one Saturday night and arrested five people for drunken driving and other offences.

"They've got to go to Dornoch for the trial," she was telling an acquaintance, hardly able to keep the excitement from her voice. "So they need drivers, and of course there are the witnesses, so altogether that's about half the village. So we decided we might as well close everything up for the day—and we're all going!"

Leaving the morals of the accused aside, I couldn't help but admire the ability of this isolated village to turn a trial case into an enjoyable day out for everyone. It was only one of the many things which impressed and fascinated me about Scotland's far north. It was a region I was very sorry to leave. In fact I would have like to stay longer, but I had to hurry. For at this point on the walk I was ruled by the calendar—winter was approaching fast, and I had to get to Cape Wrath.

Chapter 8

The North Coast

All along I had planned to arrive at Cape Wrath and turn the corner on to Britain's north coast by the end of August, and I almost made it, though not quite. On the night of August 31st I had reached Scourie, home of the northernmost palm trees in Britain. Scourie was a good two days walk from Cape Wrath, but two days wasn't really likely to make much difference to the length of the days or the likelihood of hitting bad weather. For all practical purposes I considered I was on schedule.

I had one problem, however. The difficulties of the Ardnamurchan peninsula were being repeated, in that I couldn't find out for certain whether it was possible to actually walk to Cape Wrath. There was no road to it from the south, and nothing even resembling a path. However, although desolate, the surrounding countryside was relatively flat, and I had heard of a few intrepid walkers who had set out to walk to Cape Wrath and made it. But the only one I had actually met had described the whole experience as "quite horrific", shuddered at the memory, and vowed he would never to do it again.

So I made more enquiries. But while some people told me it was known to be a relatively easy walk, others quite categorically advised me not even to attempt it. These last said that after all the rain the north-west had had recently the ground would be flooded, and they emphasised that the Cape Wrath area was extremely isolated. If I fell and broke a leg, they pointed out, nobody would ever find me. I had to grudgingly admit that this was a point to be considered.

To complicate matters still further, the area around Cape Wrath was a Ministry of Defence range, and I couldn't even find out if one was permitted to walk through it at any time, or only when it wasn't being used. It would be a nuisance, to say the least, if I walked all the way to Cape Wrath and had to come back again because I wasn't allowed through the range.

So I had things to do in Scourie other than look at palm trees. In fact, I seemed to spend all my time making phone calls to try to find out something definite about the Cape Wrath route. Finally, after contacting about three different tourist offices and driving every local official crazy, I obtained some clear and fairly encouraging information. The range, it seemed, was only used on certain days of the week, and that week it was being used on Thursday and Friday. If I kept going, I should arrive at Cape Wrath on Tuesday, and walk to Durness, the first town on the north coast, on Wednesday. So it seemed that my luck was holding out, though I would certainly have preferred to have a little more leeway.

Next, I had a mildly brilliant idea, and phoned my friend Ann in Devon. For I had suddenly remembered that she regularly took her holidays in Sheigra, northernmost village on the west coast. So she ought to know the area, and I asked her if she'd ever walked from Sheigra to Cape Wrath.

"No," Ann replied casually, "I haven't, but Owen went last year with some of my friends. Do you want to speak to him about it?"

I declined, trying hard not to laugh. Ann's son Owen was nine years old at the time. And after all the talk of it being difficult and dangerous. I decided if a boy of that age could do it, I didn't have too much to worry about.

On September 1st I left Scourie and walked to Kinlochbervie, where I stayed overnight at a guest house. From there I took the precaution of phoning the Cape Wrath lighthouse keepers to let them know what I was doing, and I asked them to send out the local mountain rescue team if I didn't arrive by the following night. This is a sensible precaution whenever one is walking alone, but one I'd never bothered with before, thinking that since I stuck to footpaths someone would be sure to find me fairly soon if I became ill or injured myself. But on the route to Cape Wrath, if I sprained an ankle or something similar, I could be out for weeks before anyone came along. And dying of exposure in North Scotland wasn't my idea of fun at all.

The lighthouse keeper listened carefully and took down all the details; he then asked me if I really wanted to go at all.

"We've got a force 10 gale up here," he said. "It's pretty wild."

That was all I needed. But I really didn't want to back out, not after all this planning, so I asked hopefully what the weather forecast was for the next day. He assured me it was supposed to be improving, but "not a lot". I decided I'd give it a try anyway.

Next morning I was up early, for it was likely to be a long day, and I took the minor roads and footpaths from Kinlochbervie to Sandwood Bay, the northernmost beach on the west coast. Here I met a bedraggled, exhausted-looking young couple, clearly heading south, laden with backpacks and camping gear. I said hello to them and asked if they'd just come from Cape Wrath.

The young man looked a bit embarrassed. "We set out for Cape Wrath yesterday," he said, pushing back a stray lock of damp hair. "But we just couldn't get there. The weather was too bad."

This wasn't encouraging news. The walk to Cape Wrath, if I managed it at all, certainly wasn't going to be a fun-filled amble. But I had rather got beyond caring about whether I was enjoying it or not. I was filled with what was, for me, unusual determination, and I decided I would just have to keep going and keep on hoping.

Sandwood Bay is an interesting place. It has a magnificent wide beach, rows of sand dunes behind, and a large inland loch from which a river flows into the sea. It would no doubt be a popular bathing beach but for its extreme northerly location and the monstrous waves which constantly pound the shore. Probably the numerous reports of ghosts in the area don't exactly help the tourist trade either, though on the other hand I suppose some people may actually be attracted by them; one never can tell. For by the loch is a ruined stone cottage, used as a bothy or shelter by hikers and mountaineers. However, it apparently requires strong nerves to do this, for past sleepers have consistently told of a bearded sailor who comes and sits on the end of the bed at night and stares at them. There are also said to be several mermaids who have been seen in the area, and I believe other strange beings too.

I didn't stop to test the truth of these stories, for I needed to reach Cape Wrath by that night if I was to be able to leave without the army taking pot shots at me. Besides, I wasn't sure I really wanted to meet this bearded sailor anyway. So after a quick look round I waded the river—not an easy operation as it was swollen from the recent rain and I got thoroughly soaked—and climbed the steep slope on the far side to the towering cliff tops beyond.

From here to Cape Wrath was only about eight miles. It should have been a relatively easy walk, for in theory all I had to do was follow the coast. However, the whole area was totally desolate, and full of bogs, streams, small cliffs and other obstacles. On top of this, I really wasn't that good at following maps, even after all this time. This was a problem I had constantly during the walk—I was fine where there were obvious features such as roads, paths, large rivers or villages; then I could find the route easily. But when I had merely the contour lines to guide me I ran into difficulties and almost invariably ended up getting lost. I'd tried everything; I'd read numerous books on map reading; I knew in theory how to distinguish a valley and a ridge, how to recognise a saddle or a spur. The books all said quite categorically that with practice one could visualise the layout of the land from looking at the contours on the map, but, try as I might, I just couldn't seem to do it. No matter how much I practised, the terrain never looked anything like I thought it should from the map. By this time I was beginning to think map reading must be like artistic or musical ability—some people do it naturally, most can do it with practice, but a few not at all. And I had decided I must be "contour-blind".

This meant that having climbed to the top of the cliffs above Sandwood Bay I had no idea exactly where I was. It wasn't too crucial in this case, for indeed all I really had to do was keep the sea on my left, but it certainly didn't make things any easier. For I didn't know how to avoid the difficult parts, and I found myself constantly scrambling up and down, wading small rivers, climbing cliffs and negotiating boggy areas. Since I couldn't see the beds of most of the streams, I didn't dare wade them barefoot. So before crossing each stream I had to take off my pack, remove my boots and socks, put on my boots again, wade across, then reverse the whole process. It was a long tiring procedure, repeated many times throughout the day.

Some of this was unavoidable, I knew, for everyone had told me the walk to Cape Wrath involved many things like this. But I felt sure if I was a better navigator it would have made things a little easier. And on top of all this, the weather was showery and cold, and the wind, though no longer gale force, was still pretty strong and persistent.

Nevertheless, on balance I enjoyed it. It is very difficult to explain why, but the unwalked countryside had a grandeur all of its own— it gave one a definite feeling of being an explorer, and this is something you can't very often experience in an overcrowded country like Britain. I soon forgot about being wet and cold. My diary for that day perhaps records my feelings most accurately; in a tired, muddy scrawl it describes the walk as "wet and boggy and spectacular and exhausting and enjoyable". All these things were possible at once; in fact, my memories are primarily of a profound feeling of elation—at being so near Cape Wrath, at seeing another almost tame deer, at feeling completely at one with my surroundings. In this sort of situation bodily aches and pains take a definite second place. This was what coastal walking was really about.

After a few miles of walking I scaled what should have been the last hill of the walk—and then I got completely lost. I've never been sure exactly how, but I think it was because I was so high up at this point that my perception of distance became confused. At any rate, I started heading towards the now visible north coast, and it wasn't until I reached the minor road leading from Cape Wrath to Durness that I realised what must have happened. Luckily I was only about two miles off course, so I staggered, by now feeling extremely tired, in the direction of the Cape Wrath lighthouse.

It is hard to describe my feelings as the lighthouse at last came into view, for I was surprised myself by their intensity. During most of the preceding six months I had merely been enjoying the walk on a relatively superficial level. As I've already mentioned, I wasn't particularly interested in fulfilling an ambition, nor did I want the great feelings of achievement people thought I must be seeking— this just wasn't the way I looked at walking, or indeed at life. And, since I'd left Sandwood Bay, I'd been so preoccupied with finding the route that I really hadn't had room in my mind for much else, consciously at any rate. But, with safety and the lighthouse finally in sight, I could relax, and when I did so the immensity of what I'd done hit me all at once.

I was actually at Cape Wrath!

I had walked the whole west coast of Britain!

To say I was pleased would be a ridiculous understatement. I wanted to tell the world. I wanted to dance and shout and give thanks to God or Nature or Lady Luck. (I believe I did do a little dancing and shouting.) At the very least, I wanted to share my feelings with my parents and Miriam.

However, this last was impossible—British Telecom has provided phone-boxes in some out of the way places, but not at Cape Wrath. So I had to content myself with telling the two lighthouse keepers, who weren't all that surprised anyway, since they fairly often met people who'd walked to Cape Wrath. Still, I staggered to their door to report my safe arrival, and asked if they had anywhere I could spend the night; I didn't fancy camping in an area notorious for its changeable weather and gale force winds. They very kindly gave me an empty room in a gutted building; it was primitive but at least it wouldn't blow away if we had another gale.

That evening I watched the sun go down from the top of the 800 foot high cliffs, the highest in Britain. It felt like the end of the world, the last outpost—I could still hardly believe I'd walked there. I wrote Miriam a letter, the nearest I could get to talking to her. She laughed when she read it, for she said my euphoria positively oozed from the pages.

Next morning I walked—or floated—along the road to the Kyle

of Durness, from where I caught the ferry over to the town of Durness. I spent the following day holed up in the youth hostel, having caught a bad cold. It wasn't a day for going out anyway; there was another gale and torrential rain. Cape Wrath was impossible to reach from any direction—the army was using the range and the ferry couldn't run due to the storms. I had just made it; again, luck had been on my side.

Durness, Tongue, Thurso—the north coast of Scotland seemed to fly by in comparison to all the weeks I'd spent walking the west coast. This was partly because it is actually very short in comparison to the long and indented west coast, and partly because it is much less mountainous. The land flattens out in the extreme north, so that by the time one reaches Caithness, in the north-east corner, the terrain is mainly open moorland. Here the local population still burn peat for fuel, so that large stacks of cut peat outside each house are a normal feature of the landscape. I was very interested in this, for when I had lived in Northumberland we had considered using the peat from the surrounding moorland instead of coal. However, we had been forced to abandon the idea because we couldn't find anyone able to teach us the correct way to cut and dry the peat; it had appeared in England to be a lost art. Now I realised all we'd have had to do was go to Caithness.

From Thurso I walked round Dunnet Head, the northernmost point of Britain. From here, on a clear day, there are good views to the Orkney Islands, and I spent a long time studying these islands through my binoculars. Soon afterwards, on September 13th, I finally reached John o'Groats.

It's a funny thing about John o'Groats. It's not the northernmost point of Britain; that honour, as already mentioned, goes to Dunnet Head. Neither is it the most north-easterly—ie Lands End's opposite number—since one can get about three miles further in that direction, to the coast at Duncansby Head. Nor, to be honest, is it particularly beautiful, as Lands End undoubtedly is. In fact, when looked at objectively John o'Groats is not particularly memorable in any way at all; it consists merely of a hotel, a couple of souvenir shops, a signpost, and a kiosk to book ferries to the Orkney Islands. This sad little collection of buildings sits on a flat, bleak stretch of land, looking slightly out of place, almost as though the buildings themselves wonder what they are doing there. There is no obvious reason for their existence.

And yet, this nondescript piece of land—it can scarcely be called a village—fascinates people, to the extent that it is one of the most visited places in Britain. Tourists come by the coachload to John o'-Groats, yet few of them even consider walking out to Duncansby Head. And of course there are the vast numbers of people who walk, cycle, turn cartwheels, or use whatever other strange means of transport they can conjure up, between John o'Groats and Lands End. They always start or finish at John o'Groats, not Duncansby Head, though the latter is the real north-east corner. It makes little real sense.

I arrived at John o'Groats quite early in the morning, since I wanted to be able to spend some time there. For, in spite of being entirely rational about it now, at the time John o'Groats had the same mystique for me as for everyone else, and reaching it was an event I had been looking forward to for weeks. I behaved like all the other tourists too—I took numerous photos, and had my own photo taken beneath the famous signpost on which one can put one's own sign or message. My signpost said, appropriately, "Brighton—by coast—3,044 miles, 13th September 1986".

Next I went to the John o'Groats Hotel, where I bought some coffee and signed the large book which was kept for long distance walkers and cyclists to record an account of what they were doing. I wrote about my walk; then I browsed through the book, finding myself quite amazed at the sheer number of people who walk or cycle between John o'Groats and Lands End. There were people leaving or arriving literally every day, though rather less walkers than cyclists, since the distance could be cycled in about two weeks and could therefore be fitted into an annual holiday.

The route had also been walked backwards, walked wearing

pyjamas, cycled on a penny-farthing—all manner of weird and wonderful stunts had been attempted. Many people were collecting money for charity and, since sponsored events are now so common, some had obviously tried to find something with a novelty value in order to attract attention. As time went on the devices used had become more and more unusual, until it began to appear as though absolutely everything had been tried. But the day I reached John o'-Groats there was something new yet again, for that day a group was about to attempt to push a truck from John o'Groats to Lands End.

I had first heard of the charity truck-pushers some days before, for their stunt had been well-publicised and had attracted a lot of attention in the surrounding area. They were a large group, included a number of unemployed young people, and were collecting for a well-known charity. However, I hadn't realised they were about to leave John o'Groats the same day as I was. It was while I was taking photos of the spectacular Duncansby rock stacks that I met two young men who turned out to be from the truck-pushing group. They told me about their proposed venture, and then they asked me what I was doing. I told them briefly about my walk and how it was going.

"Walking right round Britain?" One of them looked quite impressed. "What charity are you doing it for?"

Feeling mildly but unnecessarily guilty, mainly because of his tone of voice, I explained that I was doing it just for fun.

The man looked amazed, almost shocked, then shook his head sadly.

"A pity," he said. "That'd be worth a bomb!"

The way he said it made it sound more like a profitable business deal than anything else.

"Really," he went on. "Really a waste you not doing it for charity. You could make a fortune."

I mentioned that people who'd tried to do similar things had often been surprised at how little money they made, that the people living on the main charity walking routes, as it were, were getting rather tired of this sort of thing. Many of those living on the John o'Groats to Lands End route had told me they were too embarrassed to say so in public, but they felt as though they were being bled dry. But the truck-pusher wasn't about to listen; he seemed to have a one-track mind. Walks, to him, were to make money for charity.

I was tempted to ask what had happened to the British sense of adventure, the famous pioneering spirit, the initiative of former times? Was it all now lost beneath an admittedly well-meaning desire to make money? Was that the only purpose anyone had left for anything? Was making money obligatory? Was nobody allowed to have fun any more?

But I didn't. I'd tried similar questions in the past, when people had asked why I wasn't walking for charity, and it hadn't got me anywhere. I'd just been told I was exceedingly selfish and didn't think of others. The person concerned had then usually gone about their own business—which most of the time didn't actually involve giving to charity. I had tried telling such people that they were very welcome to give money to a charity of their choice for the number of miles I'd walked, even offered to write and tell them when I finished the walk, but this didn't satisfy them. So I wasn't about to get too involved in a discussion like this again.

So I said goodbye to the truck-pushers, and decided it was time to leave John o'Groats and Duncansby Head. I turned south, and downhill. It sounds crazy, but I had to almost literally hold myself back from running, so strong is the illusion one has of south being downhill. This illusion disappeared at the first hill I encountered, yet to some extent it remained with me. Indeed, for the next five months I always felt, somewhere in the depths of my subconscious, that it was all downhill now until the end of the walk.

The first downhill stretch led me around Sinclair's Bay and on to Wick, the largest town in this area. It seemed surprising to have such a big town so far north. I then took the main road, which follows the coast at this point, and I was surprised to suddenly catch up with the truck-pushers. There they were, twenty or thirty of them perhaps, pushing this colourfully painted truck covered in charity slogans. They looked tired already—I wondered if they'd actually make it.

I didn't really want to walk with the truck-pushers, so I turned off on what looked like a coastal footpath. It was at first, but it rapidly degenerated into a peat bog. I found myself staggering, sinking, retracing my steps, and gradually getting more and more annoyed. I was fed up with this sort of thing. I looked around wildly for the road; according to my map I should be reaching a village soon. Finally I saw a figure in the distance, with what looked like two dogs. It must be a shepherd, I thought, and I waved and yelled, terrified the figure would go away. But it didn't, and as I approached closer it turned out to be a woman of about my own age, out for a walk with her dogs. After looking rather curiously at my peat-covered clothes and generally dishevelled appearance, we began to chat, and she invited me to stay at her house in the village. I was tired and wet, and I had never been more grateful for an invitation.

Over coffee by a roaring peat fire—I hadn't realised peat gave out so much heat—Eileen told me about her life, and also gave me addresses of friends of hers I could possibly stay with further south. I finally fell asleep that night in front of the fire, vowing to stick to main roads in future.

The next day the weather was horrible—wind, rain, even some hail. I put on all my winter clothes, including fur hat and gloves, trying to cheer myself up by reflecting that at least I had less to carry that way. I stuck to the main road—I wasn't about to try any more peat bog footpaths in this weather. I stopped at a pub for lunch, just to thaw out, and that night headed straight for a guest house in Dunbeath and asked if I could stay. The owner looked at me a bit suspiciously when I told her about my walk.

"Are you doing it for charity?" she asked

I replied that I wasn't, hoping I wasn't about to get into more discussions about this; I was far too tired.

"You can stay then," she said. "But I'm not having any more charity walkers."

I asked why not.

She sighed. "It's not that I'm against collecting for charity," she said. "But there are just too many of them. You can't give to everyone. They expect to stay here at no charge because they're collecting for charity. Some of them act as though I've got no right to ask for payment. But I've got my living to earn. And why should they assume I want to give?"

Realising that for once she had a sympathetic audience, she confided: "I tell you—I've had it with this charity stuff. I can't take it any more. There should be a law against it."

I assured her I wasn't collecting for anything, and was shown to a room. I spent the evening drying out my clothes and writing articles on the walk, and occasionally thinking about the truck-pushers who were probably camping out. I certainly didn't envy them.

The following day the weather had improved and my spirits with it. I set off early, following the main road, which was now close to the sea. It was all downhill, I thought illogically as I climbed the hill above Dunbeath. Downhill to Inverness, to England, to London, and finally Brighton.

Chapter 9

The East Coast of Scotland

Like Scotland's north coast, the east coast is straight and relatively flat. Therefore it only took me ten days to walk all the way from John o'Groats to Inverness. From here I would leave the Highlands—officially at any rate—and walk almost due east across north-east Scotland.

My family and friends could hardly believe the apparent speed with which I was now moving. Was I freewheeling downhill, they would jokingly ask each time I phoned, or had I learned to fly? For the huge difference between the indented west coast and the straighter east is not obvious except on a large scale map, so to those back home it appeared as though I was now walking at an impossibly fast pace. It even seemed that way to me when I marked my progress each evening on the map, as I had since the start of the walk. I rather enjoyed filling in these long straight lines, and needing a new 1: 50,000 Ordnance Survey map nearly every day—even though it made things rather expensive.

The scenery, however, was rather disappointing after the west coast. Gone were the majestic peaks, the narrow inlets and lochs, the wild and almost uninhabited terrain. Here the main road, the A9, followed right by the coast, bringing with it people, shops, hotels, and all the other trappings of so-called civilisation. Caithness was mainly open moorland, lapped by the grey and rather dismal North Sea. The oil rigs of the Moray Firth were visible from quite far north, looming up in the middle of the sea like figures from outer space; an incongruous sight in such an area.

Since most of the time I followed the main road the walking was relatively easy, so I reached the village of Bonar Bridge, a short distance north of Inverness, within a week of leaving John o'Groats. I had planned to stop here, for I wanted to stay at the youth hostel at Carbisdale Castle. I had heard a lot about this castle, how it was built by the Duchess of Sutherland after the breakup of her marriage, just across the county boundary in Ross and Cromarty. The Scottish Youth Hostel Association had acquired the building some years earlier, but it still had much of the original furniture and was, as a youth hostel, quite unique. The castle was about four miles inland, but I was quite determined to see it—it sounded like something not to be missed.

I was pleased to find on reaching Bonar Bridge that there was another good reason for staying in the area. I was sipping coffee in a local cafe when the waitress began to chat to me.

"Are you going to the Highland Games tomorrow?" she asked.

"Which Highland Games?" I was quite surprised. For I'd now been in the Highlands about two months, yet I'd never managed to get to any of the Highland Games, try though I might. This might seem strange, for they take place just about every weekend in the summer, all over the region. But somehow I had always managed to be in the wrong place at the wrong time; I had been too early for the ones in Campbeltown, too late for those in Oban, and so on. Since it was now so late in the year, I had been fairly sure there were no more Games, so I'd even given up looking out for them. But apparently I wasn't too late after all.

"*Our* Highland Games." The waitress sounded quite proud, almost as though she were personally responsible for the Games. "They're the last ones of the year, here, tomorrow."

So at last I had made it; I was in the right place at the right time. I could visit Carbisdale Castle and go to the Highland Games, and I was really pleased.

I caught the postbus inland to the youth hostel, the first time I'd done such a thing on the walk. Postbuses are common in the Highlands, and in isolated areas they take passengers along with the mail, providing public transport where it is badly needed. Admittedly the service is slow, but nevertheless it gets you there.

In this case, however, "Postbus" was something of a misnomer.

The postman arrived in an ordinary four-seater saloon car, and looked somewhat dismayed at the four waiting potential passengers, three of them with large backpacks and obviously bound for the youth hostel. He handled the situation well, however, making the best of it and somehow managing to get us all in.

So with backpacks in the boot and the mail on our knees we commenced a slow and thorough tour of the countryside. It took us over an hour to cover the four miles to the youth hostel, since we stopped at almost every cottage and farm, for the postman either to deliver mail or pass the time of day, or more often both. I would recommend postbuses as a way of seeing the countryside, but certainly not for anyone in a hurry.

At length we arrived at the Castle. I had wanted to look around, but on discovering that the hostel had a laundry room with washing machine and dryer, the first thing I did was to wash all my clothes.

For laundry was always something of a problem on the walk, and at this point I had nothing left at all that was even remotely clean. I caused some amusement as I wandered around the hostel in a pair of waterproof over-trousers and a down jacket—with absolutely nothing on underneath.

I was entirely unprepared for what happened next. My washing completed, I put on some clothes and left the women's dormitory to go downstairs. The castle was large, and I couldn't remember the way I'd come up, so I wasn't too surprised to find

Carbisdale Castle Youth Hostel

109

myself descending an unfamiliar staircase. I was admiring the magnificent stained glass window above it, when I found myself entering a long and imposing hall full of white marble statues. It was like something out of a really first-rate museum; I'd certainly never seen anything like it in a youth hostel. In fact, this couldn't be part of the youth hostel, I decided, feeling rather alarmed. I was quite sure I must, somehow, have entered an area which was private, and I began to look for a way out. But there didn't seem to be one, apart from the staircase by which I had arrived.

Suddenly I saw a sign about halfway down the hall, almost hidden behind an intricately carved statue of what looked like a Greek god. I made for it with a feeling of relief, for to tell the truth I was beginning to feel rather out of place in this hall. But when I saw what the sign said I began to laugh, for there, right in the middle of this awe-inspiring hall, was a sign in large letters: "Broom Cupboard".

In similar fashion, the rest of the castle was an interesting mixture of impressive luxury and down-to-earth practicality. The women's dormitory was in the Duchess of Sutherland's suite, and much of her original furniture had been retained. However, the room was filled with about twelve two-tier bunk beds. In the common room, similarly, exquisite antique furniture mingled with sturdy modern armchairs. The place was fascinating, and I was impressed by what a wonderful job had been done in converting the building to a youth hostel yet still retaining so much of its original character and flavour.

The next day I returned to Bonar Bridge for the Highland Games. It was warm and sunny, and I thoroughly enjoyed watching the caber tossing and hammer throwing, listening to the pipe band, and admiring the traditional dancers. I was about to leave in the late afternoon when an acquaintance from the youth hostel called to me:

"Would you like to be in the ladies' tug o'war team, Helen?"

"What?" I hadn't bargained on taking part in the Highland Games, and I'd never been in a tug o'war in my life.

My fellow hosteller explained that there was only one ladies' team present at the games, and they needed opponents. So the youth hostel had promised to make up a team to oppose them, but they were still one person short, she told me; would I like to join them?

The next thing I remember is being knee-deep in mud, wearing studded boots which were several sizes too big, having been borrowed from one of the men's teams. I was hanging on to a large rope with all my strength, but with very little idea as to what I was actually supposed to do, except keep hanging on to it. I think this was all any of us knew, yet in spite of our complete lack of technique or team coordination our impromptu team acquitted itself rather well. We tried hard, hung on grimly, and although we eventually lost we at least succeeded in making the field significantly more muddy than it had been before. I was ridiculously happy—I had not only finally made it to the Highland Games; I had actually taken part in them.

Next day, my arms somewhat stiff from the tug o'war (it made a change from having sore legs), I set out again for Tain, where I spent the night; then Cromarty, and soon after that I reached Inverness. This was the largest town I'd been in for several weeks, and though it is really quite small, to me it seemed enormous in contrast to the rest of the Highlands. I had quite a hard time getting used to the people, shops, and traffic after so long away from them. However, I needed to make the most of being back in civilisation, for one of the first things I had to do was to find out how I could get my boots resoled. For these, my second pair of boots, were now worn down completely and had virtually no heels left. Other walkers used to look at them in amazement, for it is virtually unheard of to wear down a pair of Vibram soles in this way. But I'd done it, and I had to find a specialist repairer who could replace Vibram soles, which I hoped to do while in Inverness.

However, there turned out to be absolutely nobody in the town who could do it. I was beginning to wonder if I should ditch my boots and get some training shoes, when at last I was given the name of a man in Aberdeen who did boot repairs. I thought my boots might just make it to Aberdeen if I was lucky, so I phoned the man and asked him how long the repairs would take once I got there. I had yet another memorable phone conversation.

"About two weeks." The voice on the other end of the phone sounded calm and unhurried, and my heart sank. This relaxed attitude was all very well, but I really couldn't spend two weeks in Aberdeen.

I took a deep breath, put another coin into the phone, and considered. Could I get special treatment as a round Britain walker, I wondered? I would try.

"I'm walking round the coast of Britain," I told the man. "I really need the boots."

I got no further.

"Are you?" The voice now sounded most interested. "I'd love to do something like that. I'd really like to hear about it."

My plan seemed to be working, but as I shoved my umpteenth ten pence piece into the insatiable phonebox I reflected that I'd really have to find some other way of contacting people round the country—I must be virtually keeping British Telecom in business all by myself.

"Can I tell you about it when I get to Aberdeen?" The urgency must have shown in my voice, for I was running out of coins for the box. "You see, I'm in a phone box in Inverness and..."

"Right!" The man could obviously hurry when he needed to. "I can fix your boots in forty-eight hours when you get here. And tell me about the walk. See you soon."

As he hung up I reflected with amazement, for the hundredth time, on the difference in people's attitudes when they found out I was walking round the coast of Britain.

Inverness was memorable mainly for its tales and legends. First, of course, was the Loch Ness monster. I took a trip to Loch Ness and visited the Monster Exhibition, and I also looked out for Nessie herself. But I had no luck, though it was so foggy the day I was at

Loch Ness that she could have been basking fifty feet from the shore for all I knew.

Perhaps even more interesting than the monster, though less well-known outside the Inverness area, is the legend of the Brahan Seer. This soothsayer was burned at the stake several hundred years ago, and since that time many of his predictions have turned out to be disturbingly accurate. One of these says that if ever there are seven bridges over the River Ness, "Inverness will run red with blood". People told me that at one time a seventh bridge was being built but, mindful of the seer's predictions and taking no chances, the builders dismantled an old bridge before the new one was completed.

I thoroughly enjoyed my stay in Inverness, but finally, on September 27th, I turned East, leaving Inverness and the Highlands. I was sad to go, for Northern Scotland had become my favourite part of Britain.

As I walked across Scotland's North-East coast I began to feel that the coast of Britain was getting quite crowded. For it was here that I suddenly began to meet and hear about other coastal walkers.

There were quite a number of us walking round the coast of Britain in 1986. To my knowledge there were four people on this route at approximately the same time, plus a couple who began soon after I finished my walk. Not enough to start causing any overcrowding or soil erosion, but all the same a surprising number for one year, considering that only a handful of people had ever done the walk before.

I had heard about most of these previous walkers either before I began my own walk, or at some time during it. For there seems to be a kind of long distance grapevine, so that information about people doing any walk like this quickly became common knowledge in walking circles. I was surprised at how many people had heard about me, as a result of this grapevine, even before I'd had any publicity whatsoever.

The first coast walker of 1986 that I'd actually met had been Ron

Bullen, as I've already mentioned. But the first one I had heard about had been a young woman called Vivienne Ibbott. I never managed to meet Vivienne; in fact in one of my *Croydon Advertiser* articles I dubbed her "The Phantom Coastal Walker", so elusive did she appear to be. My first indication of her existence and planned walk had occurred very early on, just before I left Brighton. John Lees, ever on the lookout for publicity, had telephoned the TV station in Southampton to see if they would like to cover the start of my walk, and he had returned from making his call with a disbelieving expression on his face.

"Helen!" John had sounded quite upset. "They say they've got their own girl. She's leaving from Southampton, on the same day as you."

I could hardly believe it myself, though it didn't really worry me. The odds against such a coincidence must have been astronomical. I asked John for more details, but he hadn't been able to find out anything else; indeed, he seemed too stunned by the knowledge to be able to think clearly.

Personally I wasn't upset or annoyed, for I'd never particularly wanted to do something unique. Indeed, my predominant feeling was one of excitement, and from that point on I was determined to meet Vivienne. I didn't seem destined to manage this, however. In fact, for a while I wondered if she existed at all, for I heard no news about her whatsoever, although I asked wherever I went. My first real indication that she was truly walking the coast didn't occur until I reached Saundersfoot, in Pembrokeshire, South Wales. There, in the local camping shop, the proprietor greeted me with the usual and by now boring statement.

"That's a big pack you've got," he said brightly.

I was in a good mood, so I didn't ignore the predictable comment as I so often did.

"It's not really that big," I explained. "You see, I'm walking right round the coast of Britain …"

I stopped in mid-sentence, wondering why the man had nearly fallen through the floor with surprise, as it wasn't that strange, but it turned out that he had had almost the identical conversation, about ten days before, with Vivienne.

So gradually I had pieced together news of the Phantom Walker. She had indeed left Southampton on March 1st, walking clockwise as I was. She was apparently about my size, and had a large back-pack much like mine. However, she was younger than I was, and either much fitter or taking a lot of short cuts, for she was gradually getting further ahead of me. Indeed, I soon gave up all hope of ever catching her up, for by the time I reached North Wales she was about three weeks further on. I thought perhaps I might catch up with her on the west coast of Scotland, where I took so many short cuts, but there I lost her trail altogether.

So it wasn't until now, in North-East Scotland, that I finally heard of her again. She had been seen near Wick, I was told, at first. Then, soon after leaving Inverness, I found out how to contact her, for she had left her address with a local paper who had interviewed her. I wrote to her at once, but I didn't get a reply until after I arrived back home. Finally, in March 1987, I received a letter from Vivienne, tell-ing me that she had finished her walk, but with a number of short cuts and the use of some public transport in towns. Until receiving my letter she had never heard of my existence, and she wished she had known I was following so close behind.

It was at about the same time, in Portknockie, an isolated village in North-east Scotland which I reached a few days after leaving In-verness, that I met the fourth of the 1986 coastal walkers. Paul Dyer had begun his walk at John o'Groats just a day after I had left there. He had been amazed to hear that I'd just gone through, and was quite determined to meet me. Putting on a burst of speed only pos-sible while one is still fresh at the start of a long walk, he finally caught up with me, literally entering the village shop in Portknockie just after I had left it. And so we met.

I spent the next few days bumping into Paul in all sorts of places. We met over lunch in the pub at Pennan, a village famous for being the location of the film "Local Hero". He walked past the campsite where I was staying as I packed up my tent one morning, and we met on the road near Macduff. It never occurred to either of us to walk together, though I think we were both quite pleased to keep running into each other. This surprised many people, who felt sure a lone walker must want company, but it is really very difficult to do a long distance walk with another person. You need not only to get on extraordinarily well, but also to walk at approximately the same pace.

Finally, at Fraserburgh, I lost track of Paul. I heard occasional news about him afterwards from various people, and several months later received a postcard from him, from Brighton, saying that he was well and still walking.

I spent the first half of October walking the sandy beaches of Scotland's east coast in a delightfully warm Indian summer. Newburgh to Aberdeen was the longest stretch of beach I encountered on the whole walk—fourteen miles of golden sand. I continued south to Dundee, crossed the Tay Bridge, and walked through the picturesque villages of Fife. I was extraordinarily lucky, for the beautiful sunny weather continued, and I was able to enjoy sleeping under canvas right up to mid-October. Then, as I neared Edinburgh, I met another long distance walker.

Some time before, among the many invitations I received to stay with people who lived on my route, had been one from Hamish Brown, a hill walker and writer who is well-known in walking circles. Since I don't actually read many walking books I had heard of Hamish only slightly, and I hadn't read any of his books. But I was delighted at the chance of staying with another walker, and one who was something of a celebrity at that. Still, I decided maybe it might be a good idea to at least have a glance at one of Hamish's books before I reached his home, for I didn't want to appear a complete ignoramus. But good bookshops are rare on Scotland's east coast, and I reached Kinghorn, where Hamish lived, still having not read a word he'd ever written. Oh well, I thought, not too worried. I wouldn't have to tell anyone; I could bluff and pretend I'd read them, or say nothing.

The door to the cottage in Kinghorn was opened by a smiling bearded figure in breeches and sweater, and I didn't need to be a detective to identify Hamish Brown. As he held out his hand, the Shetland sheepdog behind him leaped at me, wagging his tail joyfully in greeting. I love dogs, and I reached out a hand to pat him.

"Oh what a lovely dog," I said innocently. "What's his name?"

I really shouldn't try any subterfuge—I'm no good at it; I had just given myself away completely. For Storm, Hamish's beautiful and extremely photogenic dog, was at that time even better known than Hamish himself, being featured in almost every photo in all of Hamish's books. Indeed, Hamish told me later that he himself was always recognised in youth hostels because of Storm, for "one bearded hiker looks much like another, but there's only one Storm."

So I had to give up pretending to be knowledgeable about Hamish's books. Anyway it wasn't really necessary; Hamish welcomed me as I was, and I spent a most enjoyable evening. He turned out to be a most excellent cook, and within ten minutes of my arrival I was presented with a steaming plate of haggis, turnips and potatoes—my first traditional Scottish meal, after more than three months in Scotland.

I always liked staying with other walkers, for they knew exactly what was needed. They didn't ask, "What do you want first—a cup of tea, a bath, or a meal?" They just provided all of these in quick succession.

I also thoroughly enjoyed meeting someone else who walked for pleasure, not to gain records, and we compared notes late into the evening. One thing which greatly amused Hamish was the fact that "The Guinness Book of Records" had the record for walking round the coast classified as "The Longest Continuous Walk in Britain". Obviously they didn't want to get involved in the continuing arguments as to what was or wasn't the coast. Hamish had rubbed his hands in glee when I told him this.

"Why don't you just carry on walking?" he suggested. "When you get back to Brighton, walk from Lands End to John o'Groats or something. Just make sure you walk further in all than both John

Merrill and Ron Bullen. It'd drive them crazy to be beaten—and by a woman too."

I had to admit the idea appealed to me, and I'm sure I could have done it. But I really couldn't be bothered to get involved in the record beating game, not for any reason whatsoever.

Next day, Hamish and Storm accompanied me across Kinghorn's magnificent sandy beach, and soon after I crossed the Forth Road Bridge. And that night I stayed with yet another long distance walker.

Kathy Murgatroyd was the first woman to climb all of Scotland's Munros (peaks of over 3,000 feet) in one expedition. Her record was almost unknown, for she had an absolute horror of fame, feeling sure she'd never be able to handle it. Thus her feat was not publicised at all—she was the ultimate "fun" walker. However, when she heard about me Kathy decided she had to meet "another woman who does this sort of thing" and she wrote to me explaining who she was, not realising that at that point I hardly knew what a Munro was. Still, I had been most interested to meet another woman walker, so I had replied, and we met and got on extremely well. We had a lot in common, not surprisingly, and it was again a relief to stay with someone who knew just what tired walkers needed.

The last long distance walker I was to meet, some months later, was Vera Andrews, the only other woman to have walked round the coast at that time, to my knowledge. "Granny Vera", as she was known, had written a book about her trip, from which I got her address. I wrote saying I'd like to meet her, and I stayed with her later in the year at her home in Clacton-on-Sea. Again, we got on really well, even telling the local paper in Clacton that we planned to walk round America together. And maybe we will…

By the time I left Kathy Murgatroyd's home, feeling physically and mentally much refreshed, I was almost out of Scotland. I walked through Edinburgh, where I had lived many years before, then along the beaches at Gullane and North Berwick. Soon I reached the dramatically beautiful St Abbs Head. And on October 30th I crossed my last border—back into England.

Chapter 10

The North-East of England

I was finally back in England. A large sign on the A1 proclaimed this fact, and when I reached Berwick-on-Tweed I saw all the old familiar English banks and supermarkets again. I had walked round the whole of Scotland. It had not been at all difficult on a day to day basis, but looking back it was hard to believe it had been possible.

I stayed overnight in Berwick and then headed south. Over the next few days I walked past the Holy Island causeway, and on to Bamburgh, Seahouses, and Alnmouth. This part of the Northumbrian coast is wild, bleak and beautiful; the haunt of numerous seabirds but very few people, for only occasional tourists and a few intrepid walkers and birdwatchers make it up here, especially in late autumn. The wide expanses of beach and sky are punctuated, at surprisingly frequent intervals, by castles—Bamburgh, Lindisfarne, Dunstanburgh, Warkworth. These are reminders of the bloody history of these barren shores, and I found it didn't require much imagination to picture hordes of Vikings landing on the beaches and scaling the windswept hills.

One of the most fascinating things about walking round the coast of Britain was the constant change of scene. I rarely had the same type of landscape for more than a day, so it never had the chance to become monotonous. This part of the coast was no exception; soon I reached the desolate sands of Druridge Bay, then I was almost instantly transported into the industrial north-east, as absolute a contrast as is possible. First came Lynemouth Colliery, with its completely black beach, the first of many beaches polluted by coal. Here I saw men from the nearby town of Newbiggin collecting sea-coal for resale. I had bought sea-coal when I lived in Northumberland some years earlier, but I'd never seen it collected before, and I decided to stop and ask about it. I approached one of the men; he was leading his horse and cart, and shivering in spite of being warmly dressed, for the bleak November wind was biting and cold. He seemed quite happy to stop for a while and chat to me.

"Do you get a lot of coal here?" I asked.

"Quite a bit," he told me, stamping his feet to keep warm and indicating the sacks he had collected.

Since he seemed quite friendly, I enquired further:

"Make much out of it?"

His manner changed instantly. Almost imperceptibly, but quite definitely, he became suspicious. I realised I had touched on a forbidden subject. Outwardly, however, he shrugged nonchalantly.

"It's a living," he grunted casually, yet at the same time making it quite clear he intended to say no more. He obviously wasn't about to divulge the secrets of the black economy—black in all respects—to a stranger. And it was clear the conversation was at an end.

I will remember the north-east of England for many things, but most of all for its own unique brand of friendliness. The people here say just what they mean, with no disguise or deception; they call a spade a spade. In addition, the north-east has been economically depressed for a long time, so its people understand frugality, and in no way look down on someone who is short of money or on a tight budget—to them this is a way of life. So that when, on arriving in Newbiggin, I looked in vain for somewhere to buy a cup of coffee, I was told:

"Cafe, pet? They're all closed for the winter. And the hotel's expensive. Try the bingo hall, pet, they do a nice cheap cup of coffee, and it's warm in there. Play bingo too, pet, you might win something." (I didn't.)

And in Blyth, that evening:

"The hotels are expensive, pet. But there's a house down the road where some people on the dole stay. Try there."

And at this house:

"Come in, pet; 'course you can stay here. Five pounds OK, pet—can you afford it? Come in then and I'll make you a nice cup of tea."

But it was in Peterlee, in County Durham, that I discovered the true extent of north-east hospitality and its inhabitants' willingness to put themselves out to help someone.

I arrived there on a Saturday afternoon, just five minutes after the tourist information office closed for the weekend. Resisting the temptation to break down its door, I telephoned the two or three guest house addresses I had, but they were all full. I wasn't sure where I could stay, and it was far too cold to camp, so I considered going to the police station to see if they had accommodation lists. However, since my experiences at Crofty in Wales I had been a little wary of the police; the last thing I wanted was to be arrested for vagrancy. Although, I reflected at this point, vagrants at least got a cell for the night—and it would be warmer than my tent.

I needn't have worried, however; the police did have an accommodation list, and they turned out to be most interested in my walk and extremely helpful—nothing like the policeman in Crofty. One officer immediately started phoning some of the places on his list to try to find me somewhere; however, he didn't have much luck, as they were all full. As I waited, a colleague of his joined in, suggesting other places to phone. Then another officer who had just arrived began to help, and soon another, then another, and yet another.

Suddenly it began to look as though the whole of Peterlee Police Station had dropped everything in order to help me find a place to stay. I couldn't believe it; surely they had other things to do. But no, it appeared as though Saturday afternoon must be a quiet time for crime in Peterlee, for everyone in sight had turned their resources to my accommodation problem.

At length one of the officers turned to me.

"I'm afraid there's nothing in the town," he said. "How about a few miles inland?"

As I hesitated, he continued: "I can drive you out there on my way home, and I'm sure you could get a bus back in the morning."

I agreed; I couldn't do much else, for it was getting late and I really didn't want to camp. I was also reluctant to refuse any kind of offer when they had been so incredibly kind—I had never dreamt they would put themselves out in this way.

But the most surprising thing was yet to come. In the middle of his next phone call, the officer turned to me.

"The proprietor wants to know how much you usually pay," he said.

I was momentarily nonplussed; this didn't make sense. Guest houses have fixed rates; they don't change their prices for the occasion or the person.

"How much does he charge?" I asked.

The policeman told me: "He says if you've got the guts to do what you're doing you can pay whatever you like."

What on earth could I say? Luckily, I was saved even thinking about an answer for the time being, for my silence was taken as acquiescence, and the police station immediately erupted into action. A good-looking young policeman grabbed my pack and escorted me to his car. He drove me to what turned out to be an extremely comfortable country hotel, some three or four miles inland. The proprietor there welcomed me, and instantly halved his usual price for my benefit. He even gave me a lift back to Peterlee in the morning.

So a possible disaster—no accommodation and being forced to camp in November—had been turned into one of my most comfortable nights. And it became one of my most abiding memories of the kindness of the people of the north-east of England.

However, my predominantly good feelings for the north-east were slightly soured two days later. On that day I walked from Seaton Carew, near Hartlepool, through Middlesborough to Redcar, around the estuary of the River Tees.

I had been warned in advance that this would be a rough stretch. Someone in Hartlepool had told me that one man had walked almost the whole coast of Britain, only to collapse completely on the road between Seaton Carew and Middlesborough. It wasn't that it was difficult walking—far from it; it was just a flat expanse of main road. But the terrain consisted of gloomy marshland and swamps, the prevailing headwind whistled across the flat land with nothing to stop it, and the chemical works in the area constantly belched out unpleasant odours in all directions. The effect all this usually had on a walker was to cause boredom and depression—most would have preferred a 2,000 foot peak any day.

There was a strong headwind on the day I left Seaton Carew, with dismal grey skies overhead and a chill in the air. Within a couple of miles I began to feel very tired and utterly dejected, but there was nothing to do but put my head down, grit my teeth and carry on, bearing in mind it was only a few miles to Middlesborough. But the straight, monotonous road seemed to extend to infinity, and it took all of my inner strength to keep going.

At last I reached Middlesborough, which provided the only novelty of the day in the form of its transporter bridge, the only one in Britain still operating. I thoroughly enjoyed crossing what looked and felt like a moving piece of road—a strange experience. Middlesborough itself was large and crowded; I didn't see any reason to stay there long. I had intended to take the "Black Path" from there to Redcar; this is a right of way which passes right through the middle of the steel works. However, I was warned at the tourist office that it was now a favourite place for crime and muggings. I was back in civilisation, I reflected, not greatly cheered. And I took the road, which involved a long, tedious walk with nothing to recommend it, past the steel works, through depressing inner city areas, and along a large new bypass.

By the time I reached Redcar I was tired and thoroughly fed up. It wasn't encouraging to recall that I was only a few miles from where I had started that morning, for I'd spent the whole day walking round the estuary of the River Tees. This sort of thing occurred often, and I didn't mind it if there were compensations, but that day there definitely hadn't been.

To cap it all, the only guest house I could find in Redcar turned out to be appalling. It was expensive, the room was dark and dismal, the electric fire didn't work and the landlady was unfriendly. As I sat on the lumpy bed trying to read by the light of the one bare forty watt bulb, I found myself voicing a thought I had so far almost never had: "What am I doing this for? Why on earth don't I give up and go home?"

It was probably the lowest point I reached on the whole walk.

But next morning, as I ascended the hills to reach the start of the Cleveland Way, Yorkshire's long distance footpath and scene of some of its most outstanding countryside, my spirits rose along with the cliffs. Perhaps I still didn't know why I was doing it. To tell the truth I never had. But at this point I didn't care.

The Cleveland Way follows the Yorkshire coast from Filey, through Scarborough and Whitby, to Saltburn-by-the-Sea. There it turns inland and crosses the North York Moors to finish at Helmsley. My walk was along the coastal section of the Cleveland Way, and it was good to be back on a well-defined footpath again after so much road walking. And what scenery—I couldn't have had a greater contrast to the industrial north-east and the flat marshland of the Tees estuary; it lifted my flagging spirits and gave me renewed energy.

I stopped the next night at Staithes, a picture postcard fishing village with a tiny harbour and cobbled streets, its cottages clinging to the sides of the steep cliffs. Since it was now November, most of the bed and breakfast establishments were closed for the winter—this was to be a constant problem for the remainder of the walk. But I finally found a room in one of the cottages in the village and settled down for a quiet evening. Since Staithes was such a sleepy little village, it was clear there wouldn't be much excitement that night—by eight o'clock the streets were deserted and the village almost silent.

At about 9 pm I was proved to be completely mistaken about the quiet evening. As I relaxed in front of the TV with a cup of tea, there were two loud bangs. Nora, my landlady, leapt to her feet instantly, looking excited.

"That's the lifeboat," she cried. "Come on; let's go."

Not quite understanding what all the fuss was about, and rather reluctant to leave the warm room and the Nine o'clock News, I got up rather slowly and followed her into the street. There, everything had changed completely—Staithes was a sudden hive of activity. Lights were going on in all the houses, the cobbled streets were full of people, and a group of men were running full tilt down to the harbour. Curious in spite of myself, I began to hurry to catch up with Nora. We reached the lifeboat station together, along with at least half the population of the village. It had taken us only a couple of minutes, but by the time we got there the lifeboat was well out into the bay, and the villagers, many of them relatives of the lifeboatmen, were asking around to find out why it had been called out and what was happening.

Earlier I had mentioned casually to one or two people that I was writing articles for my local paper. Now I discovered that this had been exaggerated in the way rumours often are, and someone had told the lifeboat crew that I was a visiting journalist from London. I was about to put them right, when one of the men, who appeared to be in charge, came over to me with a purposeful look on his face.

"Right," he said in a thoroughly business-like fashion, before I could even open my mouth. "Let me tell you all what's happening."

Looking approvingly at the notebook in my hand, he went on:

"The lifeboat's gone to rescue a cabin cruiser which has broken down. It's three miles out at sea, and it took us …"

He paused a moment, looked at his watch, and calculated quickly.

"It took us 2 minutes and 58 seconds to get the lifeboat launched. Three minutes is our usual time, and the record is 2 minutes and 36 seconds, the night a man was drowning in the bay."

He glanced at me expectantly, and appeared satisfied as I wrote down all this information. For what could I say? I felt like a bit of a fraud, but it was hard to do anything about it at this point. Besides, I was actually delighted at being given so much interesting information without even asking for it. Usually people were a bit reticent if I started asking questions, but apparently being a journalist—even under false pretences—made all the difference.

The man continued telling me about the work of the RNLI, and I dutifully wrote it all down. Apparently the crew were all local men, and volunteers. Many of them were fishermen, but there were a sprinkling from other professions and occupations too—teachers, labourers, the unemployed. Nowadays they earned very little for their dangerous work as lifeboatmen, but in former times the pay was enough for a week's food, and when times were hard the lifeboatmen would fight each other for life jackets so as to be able to go out.

After about half an hour the lifeboat returned to Staithes. The cabin cruiser had been towed in by the Whitby lifeboat, and the Staithes crew set to work, cleaning out their boat and stowing the equipment so that they could go home. The local population gradually drifted away, and Nora and I went home. I had enjoyed all the excitement, and I was glad that I had arrived on just that evening. For since the Staithes lifeboat is only called out on average about once a month, it was quite a coincidence that I'd managed to be there.

Halfway through our second cup of tea there were two more loud bangs. Nora and I looked at each other in amazement, for this time I knew what they meant, though I couldn't quite believe it. Again? Twice in one night? We put down our cups and ran.

This was potentially more serious. A woman in the next village had fallen over the cliff and was trapped. The lifeboat had left in record time, since its crew were all ready and available, not even having finished cleaning out the boat after their first call-out. A couple of minutes after they left an ambulance arrived from the nearest large town, and the village waited expectantly. There was a lot of curious and worried gossip. Who was the woman? How had she managed to fall in a place where the cliffs were well fenced off? Was it a suicide? Had she been pushed? The speculation went back and forth for several minutes.

We never did find out how the accident had happened, but the efficient lifeboatmen returned within a few minutes. They had rescued the woman quickly and safely, and the pathetic looking blanket-swathed bundle was passed to the waiting ambulance men, who quickly roared off into the night. We heard later on the TV news that due to everyone's prompt action she recovered quickly.

It was well after midnight by the time I got to bed that night, not a recommended practice for a long distance walker. For on our return Nora made yet another cup of tea; then, her tongue loosened by all the excitement, she proceeded to tell me all about her life in Middlesborough, where she had spent her youth. For a while she had been a minicab driver at night; this can be a dangerous occupation and she had some hair-raising stories to tell. One I will never forget concerned the night when she had been driven all over the city with a knife held to her throat by a crazy passenger. Having at last extricated herself from the situation, she had radioed her base to tell them what had happened.

"Where were you, number two?" they'd demanded, not having heard from her all evening. "What kept you?"

Gasping with fright and shock, Nora had stuttered out her story, hoping for a little sympathy and reassurance. But not in Middlesborough.

"Well?" they had retorted, somewhat impatiently. "What're you so upset about? He didn't kill you, did he? So get your ass back up here and do some work!"

As I stared at the middle-aged Yorkshirewoman who was telling this tale—and laughing about it—I reflected that one should never judge either sleepy villages, or their inhabitants, by appearances.

Next day brought bright autumn sunshine and some of the loveliest coastal scenery of the whole walk. The path wound up and down the cliffs, across sandy coves, through isolated villages. About mid-afternoon I reached Whitby, where I had an invitation to stay at an international language school. It had sounded like a fascinating place, where I could meet people from all over the world, so I'd arranged to spend one of my rest days there. When I arrived, Mary, the woman who had invited me, gave me one of the school's study bedrooms. It was warm and comfortable, and I relaxed for the afternoon, looking forward to meeting all the students in the evening and finding out about them.

However, this was not to be. I never had a chance to ask the students about anything at all, for everyone wanted to talk about my walk, to the extent that it was quite impossible for me to discuss anything else. For about an hour I answered the same questions, fired at me in various accents and various standards of English. Again and again I explained why I was walking round Britain, where I'd been, which part I liked best, and so on. Mary was at first amused, then amazed, and at last sympathetic, with the way I tried to sound interested as I made the same explanation for maybe the fiftieth time. I was beginning to understand how celebrities must feel, and why so many of them avoid publicity and people. For, though outwardly I remained calm, inwardly I knew I was beginning to get annoyed. It would have to stop soon, I knew, if I wasn't to lose my temper at some point, and I really didn't want to do that.

Later that evening I finally reached the end of my patience. I had just arrived in the common room to have a quiet cup of tea with Mary before going to bed, when a young man from Switzerland approached.

"Excuse me," he asked politely, "But I'd so like to hear about your walk …"

As Mary giggled into her tea at hearing the same comment for the umpteenth time, I took a deep breath to calm myself. The polite young man couldn't help being the straw that was about to break the camel's back. I forced myself to remain unruffled.

"I'm sorry," I said quietly. "But I'm really rather tired. Maybe tomorrow."

The young man readily agreed and left. It was only later that I found out he was a long distance walker himself, and had walked many hundreds of miles in the mountains in Europe. I would have loved to hear about that, and to compare notes with him. I had turned down just the wrong person.

Here at the language school I had encountered what was to become a problem throughout the rest of the walk. I was now too conspicuous, too well-known—I was becoming a VIP. As I came nearer to completing the walk it became harder and harder to find out about other people, for everyone wanted to hear about me. While this was flattering at first, it quickly became distinctly irksome. I began to long for obscurity, and try to hide what I was actually doing. But any walkers in winter are rare, and by this time I looked extremely fit and weatherbeaten, so it was extraordinarily difficult.

Next day brought me to the isolated youth hostel at Boggle Hole, near Robin Hood's Bay, an old time smugglers haunt. Here I was the only guest, something which was to become quite common as I stayed at more hostels in the winter. The following day I passed Long Nab Lookout, where I chatted to the coastguard on duty, who had a dog and a pet goat in the lookout with him. One sees everything on a coastal walk, I reflected. Next came Scarborough, which claims to be England's oldest seaside resort. And then I reached Filey, the end of the Cleveland Way. I could hardly believe that I was nearly at Hull, and soon I would reach Lincolnshire and the Fens.

During the second half of November and the beginning of December I covered a lot of ground, firstly walking the whole length of the Yorkshire coast down to the long thin spit of land known as Spurn Head. This three mile long projection is famous for having the only fulltime lifeboat crew in the country; they live with their families in a small community near the tip of Spurn Head. It is a unique feature of Britain, and I was glad to have had the chance to see it.

From Spurn Head I walked up the north shore of the Humber, over the huge span of the Humber Bridge, and down the coast of Lincolnshire. Early December brought me to Boston; then came the Fens, with three days of walking across flat, gale-swept countryside with scarcely a tree to break the monotony. I was very relieved to finally reach Kings Lynn and the Norfolk Coast Path, another long distance walking route. I thoroughly enjoyed the quiet and peaceful coast of north Norfolk, which was completely devoid of tourists or other visitors at this time of year. I passed through no large towns or centres of population for quite a while. At last, on December 16th, I reached the thriving resort of Great Yarmouth.

Chapter 11

Approaching London: Christmas on the Trail

I spent an interesting day in Great Yarmouth. Lorna and Peter, a couple who had invited me to stay with them in response to one of my magazine ads, turned out to be keen marathon runners. Our discussions of running and walking continued far into the night, and by the time I left I was working out how I could run the London Marathon in 1988. Peter and Lorna, on the other hand, were wondering if it would be possible to run round the coast of Britain. Now that would indeed be a first, as far as I know.

From Great Yarmouth I followed the coast to Lowestoft, in Suffolk. I stopped there as I needed to phone Peter and Lorna to sort out a couple of points about forwarding my mail. Peter answered the phone.

"Oh it's you, Helen, good." he said on hearing my voice. "I was hoping you'd phone; we didn't know how to get in touch with you. Has *The Times* contacted you yet?"

"Which Times?" I asked, trying to figure out what local paper in East Anglia that would be.

"No, no," said Peter quickly, and I realised he sounded quite excited. "I mean *The Times*—The London Times. They're trying to get in touch with you."

Once I realised what he meant I was quite excited myself. I was by now used to being interviewed by local papers, to the extent that I was getting quite fed up with it. But a national newspaper was a different matter. Peter said that apparently a *Times* reporter had seen a small piece about my walk which had recently appeared in one of the Norfolk local papers, and had decided to follow it up. He had discovered I'd stayed with Lorna and Peter, and phoned Peter to try to track me down. At that point Peter hadn't had a clue where I was, but now that he had heard from me we could set things in motion, if I wanted. So he gave me the reporter's phone number so that I could arrange a meeting.

Normally it was quite difficult for me to arrange to meet people on the walk, for to plan in advance where I'd be at a particular time was more complicated than one might imagine. The logistics involved in meeting Miriam and my brother, both of whom had visited me at various times during the walk, had put me off trying to organise such rendezvous very often—I usually either ended up having to rush like mad, or spending a day in some thoroughly dismal place waiting for the person I was supposed to meet. However, the reporter from *The Times* had actually timed things rather well. For it was now December 19th, and I was scheduled to spend five days over the Christmas holiday period at Blaxhall youth hostel, near Woodbridge in Suffolk. I could easily meet him there, I would have plenty of time for interviews, and in fact it would make the Christmas holiday period rather interesting. So I lost no time in telephoning the reporter, who arranged that he and a photographer would indeed meet me at Blaxhall youth hostel on December 23rd.

I arrived in the little village of Blaxhall on December 22nd. This had been arranged several weeks in advance, for Christmas had actually presented something of a problem for me. I didn't want to go home for it and then come back and resume the walk, as many people had suggested I should; it would have felt very strange to break the continuity at this point. On the other hand, it wasn't really a good idea to continue walking throughout the festive season either. Apart from anything else, it would have been very difficult to do so with all the shops, cafes and guest houses closed up.

Staying at a youth hostel had therefore seemed an ideal solution. Many of the hostels were open over the Christmas period, and they provided accommodation, with Christmas parties, seasonal fare, and all the usual trimmings, at very reasonable rates. Blaxhall had appeared to be approximately in the area I was likely to reach at that time, so I'd booked in there, hoping I could adjust my mileage to arrive close to December 25th. These plans had nearly come to grief when I was felled for two days with a mysterious stomach upset at Hunstanton in north Norfolk; however, eventually it had worked out almost perfectly, and I arrived at the hostel on the afternoon of December 22nd.

On the morning of the following day the reporter and photographer from *The Times* arrived. After interviewing me briefly, they decided they'd like to have some photos, and of course they wanted these to be taken on a beach. So we drove off to the nearest beach, which was at Aldburgh. Interestingly enough, this was one of the few stretches of coastline I'd missed completely, since I'd turned inland just north of it to reach Blaxhall. Still, I thought, on a photo one stretch of coastline looks much like another, and the reporter and photographer seemed happy.

Afterwards everyone commented on the naturalness of the photo in the paper, but this natural photo actually took about two hours of highly unnatural posing to produce. I walked up and down Aldburgh beach time after time, soaked by the wintry drizzle, until at last the photographer was satisfied. I began to wish I'd never agreed to come, and any illusions I might have had left that a celebrity's life was fun were quickly dispelled. However, at length we were finished, and I was assured the article and photo would be in *The Times* soon after Christmas. I rushed off happily to phone my mother and anyone else I could think of who might be interested.

The feature on my walk duly appeared on December 27th, but hardly anybody seemed to see it. It was very odd; whenever I appeared in a local paper, even if it was only a two inch column of print with no picture, I was recognised for days afterwards. Indeed, when I had arrived in Lowestoft, barely a week earlier, I had been stopped in the main street by several people who'd read about me in the Norfolk local paper. Yet now, when a national newspaper printed a large photo and comprehensive article covering nearly a quarter of a page, almost nobody saw it. Perhaps no-one in Suffolk or Essex reads The Times, or maybe nobody buys newspapers just after Christmas, but I had to admit I was a little disappointed. I had actually been looking forward to being a national celebrity.

Christmas 1986 at Blaxhall turned out to be one of the best I'd ever spent. There were about twenty people staying for the holiday period—a mixture of single people, couples, and families, with quite a sprinkling of Europeans who'd come over on the ferry to Harwich, which is quite close to Blaxhall. Jenny, the hostel warden, produced an absolutely superb Christmas dinner, and also provided abundant supplies of food and drink throughout the whole holiday. There were plenty of things to do and lots of people with whom one could play board games, go for walks, or just chat. However, many people had come specifically because they wanted an active Christmas, so they were anxious to walk or cycle and explore the area. I, on the other hand, had decided to have a complete rest, and my complete and absolute slothfulness amazed many of these people.

"What are you doing today, Helen?", someone asked me on Christmas Eve afternoon.

"Not a lot," I replied, yawning. "I think maybe I'll do another jigsaw."

"But you can do that at home," replied my surprised questioner, who was dressed in his cycling gear.

"Yes," I agreed. "But I haven't been home for ten months."

And so I found myself telling the story of the walk to an enthralled audience, yet again.

By the time I came to leave Blaxhall on December 28th I felt rested, rejuvenated, and quite ready for the wintry trail ahead of me. I also felt thoroughly overstuffed with good food, and the waistband on my trousers proved beyond doubt that I had put on far too much weight over the Christmas period.

The effect of the walk on my weight and metabolism had been very interesting, to say the least. For the first few months I had lost weight almost continuously, which perhaps doesn't seem surprising in view of the amount of extremely strenuous walking I was doing. However, since I put on weight very easily I was quite delighted to be getting thinner without dieting; it was a new experience. I was so pleased about it I almost considered walking twenty miles a day for the rest of my life. In fact, after a month or two I even began to worry for the first time in my life that I was losing too much weight. For in spite of having a huge appetite, and eating three meals a day and many snacks and bars of chocolate in between, I continued to get thinner.

However, after a few months things changed. My appetite adjusted to the new way of life; I no longer felt hungry all the time, and I ate far less than I had at the start. At the same time, however, I began to put on weight! This would seem to be impossible, especially when one considers just how many calories I should theoretically have been burning off, but nevertheless it happened. People assured me that I must simply be becoming more muscular, and no doubt this was to a certain extent true, but since when have spare tyres been made of muscle? At any rate, by Christmas I was beginning to look quite obviously larger, and all my clothes were tight. And by the end of the walk I was about twenty pounds heavier than when I started.

I still can't figure out why this happened, or how, and neither can anyone else I've spoken to. The only explanation I can think of is that my metabolism as well as my appetite adjusted itself to the walk, but then it over-adjusted somewhat. It was all very puzzling, for I was certainly very fit by then, and I felt healthy and energetic, but I was definitely getting fat. Perhaps my body had in some way programmed itself for an emergency, and decided it required some food stores. No doubt if I had been in a survival situation that would have been extremely useful, but as it was I didn't like it at all.

Even when I realised what was happening it was almost impossible not to put on more weight. For by this time it was winter, and all the people I stayed with were quite determined to feed me well.

"Eat up," they'd urge, as though I was a finicky child. "Don't worry; you'll burn it all off tomorrow."

The trouble was that I didn't burn it off; it just sat there on my hips. Which accounts for the fact that when people tell me aerobic exercise burns off fat I tend to be unconvinced—for me, it quite clearly doesn't.

So it was with regret that a somewhat overweight round Britain walker left Blaxhall and walked to Woodbridge. From there I followed the bank of the River Deben to Felixstowe, where I caught the ferry over to Harwich. I was now in Essex, with just three more counties to go; only Essex, Kent, and East Sussex. I was very nearly home.

I reached Colchester on New Year's Eve, and on the first day of 1987 I was up bright and early to continue walking round the heavily indented Essex coastline. In terms of its rivers, coastal inlets, and other complications for a walker, Essex comes a close second to the west coast of Scotland. The scenery, however, is a complete contrast, being mainly flat fields and marshland. Some people find it depressing, but I liked rural Essex; with its wide skies, gentle impressionist-type landscapes and abundant birdlife it had a beauty all its own. And it was hard to believe, in some of the isolated villages, that I was barely a couple of hours drive from central London.

From Maldon I began walking round the Dengie Peninsula, a little-known projection of land between the Rivers Blackwater and Crouch. I stopped the night of January 4th at the village of Tillingham, and while I was there I phoned John Lees in order to make preparations for my return to Brighton, which Radio Sussex wanted to cover. I had by now calculated that if all went well I could easily reach Brighton by the end of the month. So John and I set an actual date—January 31st—and he promised to inform the media and make other arrangements.

The next day, at about noon, I reached Burnham-on-Crouch, a popular sailing centre, where I was fairly certain I would be able to find someone to take me across the river, thus saving a day's walk detouring round it. However, I had not allowed for the fact that in mid-winter the town is deserted and most of the boats have been taken out of the water for the season. I spent about two hours walking around, talking to people in pubs and cafes, going to all the boatyards and asking if anyone could take me across, but all to no avail; there simply weren't any boats available.

At last I realised I would have to give up. It was getting late; I had better decide what I was going to do. Should I stay in Burnham-on-Crouch for the night, I wondered, or should I try to walk further on up the river? I was just thinking about this when I noticed a man approaching from one of the boatyards. I recognised him as one of the people I'd talked to earlier, one who had assured me there were definitely no boats available.

"Hello," he greeted me. "No luck then? What are you doing here anyway? That's certainly a big pack you've got."

I was tired, and so I very nearly made some quick, conversation-ending answer. However, I stopped myself just in time; after all, he meant to be friendly. So I resigned myself to telling the long story, yet again.

"I'm walking round the coast of Britain," I began.

"Oh yes?" He sounded genuinely interested. "Where did you start?"

"Brighton."

"Oh, you haven't gone very far then."

"I have actually; I'm going clockwise; I'm nearly finished."

"Clockwise!" He paused, obviously doing some rapid mental calculation. "That must be absolutely thousands of miles! Scotland too?"

"Yes, it's about 4,500 miles so far."

"You're walking? Not hitching, or getting buses?"

"Yes, that's right, I'm walking."

"Well," he mused. "That puts a whole different light on things. Wait a moment …"

Then he called out to a man working in the boatyard, "Malcolm. Here a minute. Can you get out one of the boats and take this young lady over the river as soon as possible. I think we should help her out; she's walking round the whole coast of Britain."

So I was to get my lift. I marvelled, yet again, on the kindness of people, and their responses when they found out what I was doing.

In fact, as time went on and my total mileage increased, some people's reactions became quite strange. For now, instead of just being surprised that I was walking round Britain, many people actually refused to believe I'd walked so far. I have heard that people cannot perceive things which they believe are impossible, and I think something of this kind was happening. For some people just would not believe they were hearing right. One man actually said to me, when I told him what I was doing:

"Excuse me, I think I misheard you; I thought you said you were walking round the coast of Britain."

Most people didn't go quite this far; they merely adjusted what I said slightly to suit their own ideas or beliefs. So a typical conversation that winter went something like this:

"That's a big pack you've got; are you going far?"

"I'm walking round the whole coast of Britain."

"Oh, I see. My son did something like that; he hitch-hiked round Europe. Do you find it easy to get lifts?"

"I don't take lifts; I'm walking."

"Oh yes; on holiday are you? For a couple of weeks?"

"No, it'll take about a year. I'm walking round the whole coast of Britain."

A puzzled pause would follow.

"But you must take buses sometimes. You can't possibly walk all that way."

"No, I just walk."

"Walking? All the time? It's impossible."

These conversations were making it clear to me in a way nothing else had done that my walk was something almost unique. This seemed extremely odd to me, for after ten months the walk was becoming something quite normal; I genuinely couldn't understand what all the fuss was about.

By the time Malcolm had the boat ready it was mid-afternoon. I realised I would need to find somewhere to stay on the other side of the river, as it would be almost dark by the time we arrived. It turned out my luck was in—there was a hotel just the other side of the river which usually provided accommodation for boat owners. The proprietors told me on the phone that they were officially closed for the winter, but nevertheless I could have a room. They couldn't provide meals, and even without breakfast the room cost more than I had ever paid on the whole trip; but I decided to take it as there was really nowhere else to stay.

When we reached the south shore of the river I thanked Malcolm and made my way to the hotel. It was actually a kind of "boatel", for I was shown to a room which looked rather like a cabin on a large yacht. It was very small, but it looked comfortable and warm, and I sank gratefully on to the bed after what had been a long and eventful day.

The series of events which followed were like something out of a TV sitcom. I decided I would feel better after a nice hot shower, so I went into the adjoining bathroom and undressed. As I turned on the shower I almost leapt out of my skin as well as out of the shower cubicle; the water was absolutely freezing cold. I crouched in the far corner of the shower unit, attempting to keep dry as I fiddled with the taps to try to get hot water. But it was no good; whatever I did it was absolutely icy cold.

Finally I gave up, and decided I'd do without a shower. It was only then that I discovered I couldn't turn the thing off. Still trying to keep out of the way of the stream of icy water, taking refuge under a large towel, I turned both taps frantically. At last the water eased to a trickle, and I wrapped a towel tightly round the taps and retreated to the bedroom. Heaving a sigh of relief, I decided I'd have a cup of coffee instead, so I filled the kettle and plugged it in. However, as I put coffee into the cup I heard an ominous drip, and I turned to see a large pool of water spreading across the table and cascading onto the floor. The kettle leaked, extremely badly.

By this time I was beginning to get annoyed. Never mind, I reasoned, things weren't that bad; I could at least watch the TV. But even that was over-optimistic; for when I turned it on I was confronted first by a severely flickering picture, then sound only, and finally absolutely nothing—the TV was quite dead.

By now I had had enough. I would go to bed; nothing could go wrong there. But when I tried to open the window, so as to have some air overnight in the tiny room, the catch came away in my hand.

This was the last straw. By now I firmly believed the hotel was booby-trapped. I dived under the bedclothes and went to sleep, wondering, as I slid into oblivion, whether the place would explode in the middle of the night, or what. I knew the hotel was officially closed, but nevertheless what was happening was ridiculous.

In the morning I was relieved to discover that the room was still in one piece. Feeling more confident, I washed at the sink and made coffee with another towel wrapped around the leaky kettle. I packed up my things, then decided to use the toilet before I left. And as I flushed it, the handle came off in my hand. This was unbelievable. As I stood there, holding the toilet handle, looking at the unusable shower, the towel-wrapped kettle, the broken TV and the handleless window, I began to laugh in spite of myself. I only wished I'd had a video camera to record that night.

This was just one example of some of the more unusual nights I spent on the walk. One night I had stayed in a hotel which was reputed to be haunted. I didn't actually see any ghosts, but I did have a very disturbed and sleepless night for some reason, and I wouldn't go there again. Then there was the watersports centre where the young girl employee invited over all her friends and played heavy rock music in the adjoining room until 4 am, at which point I got up and threatened her with the tortures of the damned (or the sack at the very least) if she didn't stop. I stayed in a guest house in the Highlands where the landlady refused to let me leave without giving me a Christian tract to read, finally wrapping it around a sandwich which she gave me for lunch, so that I couldn't refuse. And there was the youth hostel where the warden collected live crabs which one was liable to find in all sorts of odd places—in the sinks, on the dining table, on shelves—everywhere. I used to check my bed before getting into it in that hostel.

Within a few months of starting the walk I had realised that in the area of accommodation you don't necessarily get what you pay for—you take pot luck. There is very little way of finding out in advance if a place is good or not, and the price gives very little indication. The booby-trapped hotel was the most expensive place I'd ever stayed in, while some of the best guest houses cost so little I still can't see how the proprietors made any profit at all.

Still, in spite of everything I left the booby-trapped hotel in a good mood. The weather was warm for January, and I was on my way to stay with an old school friend who now lived near Southend. After a day's rest with my friend I began to walk up the long estuary of the Thames. On January 9th I reached Tilbury, from where I caught the ferry over to Gravesend. This was a milestone, for I had crossed my final river; I was now south of the Thames. I was also in Kent, barely a stone's throw, relatively speaking, from Brighton. And so far I had been extraordinarily lucky with the weather; I had had a wonderful summer in the Highlands, and a warm autumn. It was now still exceedingly mild for January, with no snow and little frost as yet. So it was beginning to look as though I would have an easy, leisurely stroll round the Kent coast, taking my time so as to reach Brighton by the end of the month. At this late stage it seemed that there was very little that could go wrong.

But, as usual, I spoke too soon.

Chapter 12

South of the Thames: The Big Freeze

I reached the town of Rochester on January 10th. The unseasonably mild weather had finally changed, becoming quite wintry with some light showers of snow. But I wasn't too worried; I had expected to have some snow by mid-January, and there wasn't very much of it anyway. I found a guest house, went to sleep looking out over the River Medway, and awoke to find the view changed and the river frozen. Three inches of snow had fallen overnight in Rochester and more was forecast for that day. I decided it might be safer to take the main road rather than the footpaths, at least until I reached Sittingbourne the next evening.

The forecast had been merely for snow showers, but it snowed non-stop all that day. I kept to the main road and ploughed on, now and then looking rather nervously at the steadily thickening white sheets by the side of the road. Just outside Gillingham, on the main road, I ran into fellow coastal walker Ron Bullen again. Both of us looked somewhat like Arctic explorers, clad in our waterproof jackets and overtrousers, plus mittens, balaclavas and hoods; we scarcely recognised each other. But I was delighted to see him, and we wished each other luck with the rest of the journey, for we were now both very nearly home. I found myself laughing as we tried to juggle our mittens and bags so as to be able to shake hands, finally giving up the attempt and just saying goodbye instead.

A few miles from Sittingbourne I stopped at a cafe to have a meal and also to telephone my mother. I was worried in case she had heard the radio's dire-sounding stories about the heavy snow in Kent, and I wanted to reassure her that the snow really wasn't that heavy. In fact she hadn't been too concerned, for there was no snow at all in Croydon and she hadn't heard the reports about Kent. So she believed my description of the conditions and wished me luck with the rest of the walk.

I came out of the phone box to discover that what I had told my mother had inadvertently been a complete lie. For I emerged into a blizzard. I gazed at the white ground meeting the equally white sky with no distinction at all between them, so that if it hadn't been for the faint outline of the main road it would have been impossible to tell where I was—an almost complete white-out. I've lived in Scotland, in the hills of Northumberland, and among the mountains of Northern California, but I'd never seen anything like this. Who would have thought it possible in the south-east; in Kent, the so-called Garden of England?

By the time I reached Sittingbourne, at around 6 pm, over a foot of snow had fallen. The last few miles had been extremely hard walking, and I collapsed gratefully at the first guest house I came to. It was almost full, mainly with people who had been caught unawares by the sudden blizzard. I met a couple from Croydon whose car was stuck in a ditch, a family who had found the roads to London completely impassable, and many others with similar stories. As so often when disaster strikes, people seemed to have lost their usual inhibitions, and there was quite a party atmosphere as everyone compared notes on their own experiences in what the media was already calling "The Big Freeze".

The following morning there was over three foot of snow in Sittingbourne. It had finally stopped snowing, I was told, at around midnight. As I stepped out of the back door of the guest house I almost fell into a waist-deep drift. I staggered with some difficulty to the main road and stared in amazement. Sittingbourne was almost unrecognisable. The scene looked like something from around the turn of the century, with scarcely any cars, and crowds of people on foot. The only reminder that it was in fact 1987 was the nose-to-tail convoy of lorries all along one side of the main street, all stranded and many temporarily abandoned. Many of the newspapers showed aerial photographs of Sittingbourne that morning, for it was almost unbelievable.

Most of the roads were completely blocked, but the main trunk road was just about passable, at least on foot, so I set off. And strange though it may seem, I actually began to enjoy myself. It was a clear, sunny day, the snow had stopped, and it was fascinating to look at the beautiful Siberian-like landscape Besides, that amount of snow couldn't last long, I reasoned. It would probably melt later in the day, and it was likely to be very localised anyway.

A few miles on I reached the small village of Teynham, and here I encountered another problem. I needed to go to the toilet, and the pub and all the cafes in the village were closed. Normally in such circumstances I would have walked out of the village and gone behind the nearest bush; but this was rather difficult here, for it would involve wading through four or five foot deep snow. The only place in the village which appeared to be open was the Health Centre, so I decided to try there. I peered rather cautiously through their door, aware that I bore more than a passing resemblance to an snowman, and I wasn't sure how a waiting room full of people would react to me. But I needn't have worried; the place was almost deserted. The receptionist looked up as I came in.

"Of course you can use the toilet," she said in response to my request. "Would you like a cup of coffee too?"

I accepted gratefully, and she in her turn looked delighted to have some company. Over coffee she told me about the state of things in rural Kent. The snow wasn't just local, and the media hadn't been exaggerating; everything was almost at a standstill. The doctor couldn't get into Teynham, which didn't matter too much as none of the patients had turned up at the Health Centre anyway. The midwife, however, was very worried about a woman in one of the outlying villages; her baby was already ten days overdue, and if she went into labour now nobody could possibly reach her. A number of villages were completely cut off, and already some people were running out of food and fuel. It was a story which was to continue, and worsen, for several days, as snow continued to fall throughout Kent and Sussex. I began to appreciate for the first time the full extent to which Kent had been gripped by these unprecedented Arctic conditions. I also wondered how long I could keep on walking if this kept up. Had I been a bit premature, arranging to reach Brighton by January 31st?

That night I reached Faversham, where I had been invited to stay with the mother of Peter, my marathon-running friend from Great Yarmouth. She was very surprised to see me, but extremely welcoming, apologising profusely for the fact that I would have to sleep on the floor. For her friend Mary from Hastings was staying, since she had no way of getting home until the trains started running again, and there was only one spare bed. I waved aside her apologies, just grateful to have a roof over my head, considering the appalling weather conditions.

The next day I just went as far as Whitstable, a distance of about eleven miles. I had decided the most sensible thing was to cut down on mileage and conserve my energy, since walking in the snow was very tiring. Besides, I had many invitations to stay with people in Kent, and it would be sensible to take up all of them even if they weren't a normal full day's walk apart. That way I would gradually make progress, but without wearing myself out or getting stranded. For even the main roads were barely passable now, and there were very few cars apart from ones which had been abandoned by the side of the road. There were constant radio reports of roads blocked, motorists stranded, trains stuck, schools closed. Kent was in the grip of the worst weather of the century.

Amazingly, I was still managing to cover about fifteen miles a day. This was probably more than anyone else in Kent at that time, and I'm sure I must hold an unofficial record for distance covered during The Big Freeze. In these conditions walking was really the only way to get around. But one needed to be in good physical shape to do it, and I was thankful that I was, finally, fit enough to cope.

I stayed in Whitstable that night and Herne Bay the next. The following day I planned to reach Margate, where I had heard there was very little snow. So with luck I only had one more day of walking in The Big Freeze. However, next morning brought a new difficulty.

There were now extremely high winds, and these were driving the fallen snow into eight and ten foot drifts, causing conditions to be even colder and more dangerous than before. There were now constant warnings on the radio, telling people to "stay indoors unless your journey is absolutely necessary".

I considered staying in Herne Bay, but I really didn't want to; I couldn't think what I'd do with myself there. I didn't feel I needed a rest, and I wanted to get to Margate, safely out of the snowbound area. So I made up my mind to just walk to the start of the main road to Margate—the Thanet Way—and see how it looked. On finding that it appeared to be passable, I made my decision and set off.

The wind was extremely cold, and I was thankful that I was fit and had appropriate clothing, or I doubt if I'd have been able to make it. It was very hard going, in any case. But I wasn't really worried; I knew that I could cope with most conditions, as I'd already done so.

About a mile out of Herne Bay I was surprised by a police van which drew up alongside. I automatically stiffened, remembering the radio warning to stay indoors unless your journey is absolutely necessary. Half expecting the police to order me off the road, I began to defend myself vehemently before they could utter a word.

"I know I'm mad; you don't need to tell me. But I'll be alright, really; I'm only going as far as Margate. You see, I'm walking round the whole coast of Britain. And I'm very fit and I've got good equipment, and I know what I'm doing, really I do."

I paused for breath, then added, almost as an afterthought: "By the way, is the road open?"

The policemen began to laugh. They assured me the road was indeed open, and made no effort to stop me walking, simply telling me about the road conditions and wishing me luck. Actually I think I made their day. Also, I think it was obvious to them that I was properly equipped for the conditions and knew what I was doing. I was now a very different person, in that sense, from the young woman who'd left Brighton in a snowstorm so many months before. In my ten month walk I had gained a great deal of experience, a number of extra clothes, and above all—if somewhat belatedly—a high degree of physical fitness. All these made walking in these extreme conditions possible, safe, and even enjoyable, rather than highly dangerous.

I reached Margate in late afternoon. The reports had indeed been true; there was barely an inch of snow and little wind. I had made it through The Big Freeze. I was slightly behind schedule, but nothing I couldn't catch up, as I had allowed a few extra days to reach Brighton anyway. With a reasonable amount of luck I could still get there by January 31st as planned.

On January 16th I rounded the North Foreland, my final corner. There was nothing there to signify that this was one of the four corners of Britain; no tourist paraphernalia like that at John o'-Groats and Lands End, no dramatic scenery like the moorland and cliffs of Cape Wrath. But to me it was one of the highlights of the walk, for I was now back on the south coast and less than 200 miles from Brighton. I knew that it was ridiculous to talk of four corners in a completely non-rectangular country like Britain, but still I felt as though the North Foreland was a great milestone, and I felt like singing and dancing as I walked along the seafront to Broadstairs. It wasn't exactly joy I felt, neither was it triumph or a feeling of achievement; indeed it is hard to precisely put a name to my feelings. I think maybe a sense of wonder was foremost in my mind that day. I had walked right round the coast; was it really possible? Even to me it seemed unbelievable that I had done it, probably because at this point I could look at it objectively, as though it was someone else who had done the walk. Looked at in this way it seemed nothing short of a miracle; how could an ordinary woman, of no great physical ability, simply stroll round the coast for nearly 5,000 miles?

I spent the following night at Ramsgate with Teresa, a young woman who had invited me to stay in response to one of my ads, who was to become a good friend. It had been Teresa who had assured me there was hardly any snow in Margate when I had telephoned her from the snowbound areas of Kent several days earlier.

"The coastal path's quite clear," she had said. "I run that route regularly, round the coast to Margate and then back to Ramsgate on the road. I did it on Sunday and it's fine."

It was only later, when I looked at the map to plan my own route, that I realised just what Teresa had said. From Ramsgate to Margate around the coast was over ten miles, and by road back again was only slightly less. Was this woman a marathon runner or something?

It turned out that indeed she was, with a string of marathon successes under her belt and a collection of cups and trophies on her mantelpiece. I have yet to find out why it was that so many marathon runners invited me to stay; possibly they felt some kind of kinship with me. At any rate, in Ramsgate I enjoyed yet more discussions and comparisons of long distance running and walking.

I was hoping things would be peaceful now that I had come through The Big Freeze, but Ramsgate turned out to be the scene of yet another disaster; the night I arrived there was a major power cut. So while a large area of Kent still lay snowbound, Thanet was plunged into complete darkness for hours. I really began to wonder if the world would ever get back to normal.

The next morning I set off for Deal, and the following day I reached Dover. Just east of Dover, at the village of St Margaret's at Cliffe, the snow began again; apparently only the Isle of Thanet had missed The Big Freeze. In fact, the snow started quite suddenly on the cliff path between St Margaret's and Dover, so that I suddenly found myself falling into four and five foot drifts on the path. This made progress very slow and difficult, and I realised I would have to stick to roads again from then on.

From Dover I carried on to Folkestone, then down the coast to Dungeness and on to Lydd. This small town is now several miles from the coast, but it used to be a port and also a smuggling centre. There are numerous stories about Lydd's smuggling heydey, one of them telling of over six hundred mules leaving the town with the smugglers' spoils.

From Lydd I continued on west. I walked through Rye with its narrow cobbled streets, then Winchelsea, the smallest town in Britain, finally reaching Hastings on January 25th. Here I had yet another invitation to stay with people, and I took a day off, which I felt I really needed. For I was beginning to realise just how tired I was. This fatigue was not so much physical, for I was very fit, and even walking in the snow hadn't been too difficult. It was more as though a kind of long-term weariness was settling in right to my bones, and this was at least as much mental as physical. I was tired of continually having to plan my route, arrange places to stay, organise things so that I could eat and sleep and keep warm. For now that it was winter I could no longer eat by the roadside and sleep under the stars, at least not safely and enjoyably, and all this organisation took a great deal of time and energy.

I was also, rather surprisingly, tired of meeting so many people. Staying with so many different people was becoming a strain and beginning to take its toll. While I was extremely grateful to everyone who invited me to stay—indeed, I doubt if I could have finished the walk without all the help and hospitality—it was starting to produce stress of a type that I had not expected. For I constantly had to be friendly and sociable, to fit in with different ways of life and ways of doing things, no matter how I felt. No matter how tired I was, I had to continually tell the story of the walk over and over again, answer the same questions about it, and try to sound as though I was interested and enjoying the conversation. I really couldn't visit people I'd never met, who had been kind enough to offer me hospitality, and just say: "Sorry, I don't feel like talking. I just want a bath and a meal and a chance to be by myself, and I'll be off first thing in the morning, thank you very much." Yet this was what I was beginning to want, and need, to do. I really longed for privacy and a chance to be alone. The constant need for socializing was turning out to be a drawback, and this was quite unexpected for me, for earlier in the walk I had actually wanted to meet people, indeed it had been one of the main purposes of the walk.

Many people asked me if I ever felt lonely on the walk, yet during these last few weeks quite the reverse was true. I found myself longing to have some time to myself, to be in my own place, to do as I liked when I liked. I was beginning to be weary, not of walking but of travelling, of being "on the road", with its attendant lack of privacy and the constant change and adaptation it required. Eleven months was a long time; I felt in need of a break.

When I left Hastings I walked to Bexhill and Eastbourne, then round Beachy Head. The Big Freeze was over, the snow had melted, and I found that in spite of the weather and my own fatigue, I was actually ahead of schedule. It was not a problem, however, for I had allowed for this possibility by arranging to stay with an old school friend who now lived in Hailsham, a few miles inland. So from Beachy Head I followed the spectacular path across the Seven Sisters, one of the most memorable walks of the whole trip. Though I still maintain there are eight sisters, and I counted them.

My friend Anne picked me up in Seaford and took me to her house for a couple of days rest. It was good to see her and a relief to be staying with somebody I knew well, with whom I didn't have to stand on ceremony at all. It meant I could have a complete rest, and also begin to make detailed arrangements for my return to Brighton. It was now January 27th, and I was very nearly back. I started to make final preparations for my return, phoning friends and relatives, getting rid of clothes I didn't need and washing those I would wear, and generally getting organised. For there were only four days left.

Chapter 13

Brighton Again: a 5,000-mile Amble Completed

On the day before my planned arrival in Brighton I left Seaford early. I had decided to stay at Rottingdean that night; this would give me a nice easy five-mile walk into Brighton the next day. I wanted to arrive looking as though it really had been a relaxed 5,000 mile amble, even though in reality this hadn't always been the case.

I arrived in Rottingdean in the afternoon and found somewhere to stay. I then put through a call to Radio Sussex.

"Can I speak to John Lees please?"

As soon as they heard who it was, John was on the line almost immediately.

"Helen, how are you? Where are you phoning from?"

"Rottingdean," I replied. "Five miles down the coast. I can see the Palace Pier."

"Rottingdean!" John sounded as though he could hardly believe it, though he had known for several weeks that I would be arriving in Brighton at the end of January. But he hadn't heard from me for a while, and perhaps he thought I'd vanished under a snowdrift in the Big Freeze.

Actually, I could hardly believe it myself. When I'd first seen the Palace Pier in the distance, having left it so many months ago, it had seemed impossible. I hadn't been able to take my eyes off it as I walked along. Could it really be there in front of me? Was it real?

John paused for scarcely a second, then said: "OK, hold on; we're just about ready. Alright if we do an interview with you right now?"

I agreed, for we had tentatively arranged this some days earlier.

In any case, radio interviews no longer made me nervous; they were purely routine now that I had done so many. And this one I was rather looking forward to.

There was a pause while the radio station arranged things at their end, then John was on the line again, putting on the studiedly casual yet slightly artificial tone of voice which all radio interviewers seem to habitually adopt.

"Helen, how does it feel to have walked right round the coast of Britain?"

"Well …" I thought quickly, trying to find exactly the right words to explain how I felt, which wasn't easy. I wanted to be honest about it, not come up with any of the expected cliches about having a wonderful sense of achievement, or the usual jokes about sore feet. So after a moment I told them: "I feel as though I've proved to myself beyond any doubt that Britain is an island."

There was a pause at the other end, and I suddenly realised how odd it must sound. Yet for me it summed up better than anything else the emotions I had experienced when I'd first seen the Palace Pier ahead of me, after having left it behind me all those months ago. It could only be where it was, logically, because I had walked right round an island. The sight of the pier had brought home to me, for the first time, what I had actually done. Before that it had felt like a long walk, nothing more.

John, however, obviously didn't really understand all this, or the implications of what I'd said. Sounding slightly bemused, he tried again:

"You must have a tremendous feeling of achievement."

I thought for a moment.

"No," I replied, wanting to be absolutely honest. "Not really. But perhaps it hasn't hit me yet. I don't think I've quite taken it in."

"How many miles have you walked altogether?" John was now on easier ground.

"Four thousand, nine hundred and twenty two," I replied. I had worked this out the night before. I'd very much wanted to do over

5,000 miles, but short of walking in circles round the Isle of Thanet, it would have been impossible.

"Is this a record?" John asked.

"I don't know yet," I replied. "I think so. But it's up to *The Guinness Book of Records.*"

So the interview was all a bit inconclusive. I suppose everyone would have been happier if I'd said it had been incredibly difficult and it felt absolutely wonderful to know I'd done it, but that wasn't my way. I was still just a wanderer, a long distance ambler. If I'd broken a record, that was fine. But I didn't really want to make a big deal out of it.

I was also very tired, and soon after the interview I decided to get ready for bed. But it took me quite a while, for first I had to phone *The Times* since I'd promised to let them know when I was arriving in Brighton, and after that the BBC. Then John Lees phoned back again, with a request.

"Helen," he said earnestly. "Would you paddle in the sea when you get to Brighton, so we can get some photos?"

"I don't know about that." It was mid-winter, and freezing cold.

"You see," continued John. "It would sound really good if you said 'Now I just want to dip my feet in the Brighton briny' and then got photographed doing it. The papers would really like that."

"No way," I said. "I don't talk like that anyway."

"But it would get you more publicity."

"I really don't care. I don't think I want that sort of publicity."

So we left it.

The couple who ran the guest house in Rottingdean had given me a room when I arrived, glad to have any guests at all in mid-winter. But I don't think they'd bargained on having let the room to a minor celebrity, which is what I seemed to be at this point. They appeared amazed by it all, and I think they thoroughly enjoyed it too. They also very generously offered to put me up for the night at no charge. So on my last night I had proof, if I needed it, that there were generous and friendly people in the south-east as well as the rest of the country.

Next day I was off bright and early, for in spite of the fact that I only had five miles to walk it was to be a busy day. I was due to reach Brighton at 11 am, and John had arranged for representatives from a number of newspapers—both local and national—plus the TV stations, and of course Radio Sussex, to all be there. One of the hotels in Brighton had offered to put on a champagne reception, and British Rail had offered me a free train ticket back to Croydon. Many of my friends and relatives were planning to meet me as well—it was going to be quite a homecoming.

So I left early, to allow myself plenty of time. I really wanted to savour the last few miles alone. I still couldn't get over seeing the Palace Pier in front of me. It was a sight I had looked forward to for many months, and I wanted to be able to enjoy these last few miles quietly, without interruption from anyone,

The first two or three miles were as peaceful as I could have wished, enabling me to take my time and get used to the idea that I had walked round the whole coast of Britain, and after a while the novelty wore off. Then a couple of miles from Brighton I saw a familiar figure coming towards me. There was no mistaking that brightly coloured poncho and wild untamed hair—Miriam. I was absolutely delighted to see her; we hugged each other and danced around like a couple of kids. This was the end of my time to myself, but by now I didn't mind.

It was just as well that I didn't, for barely half a mile further on a Radio Sussex newscar drew up, with John Lees and a colleague; they congratulated me and asked if I'd do a final last minute interview. And just as I finished passing on my feelings to all the south coast listeners, a car screeched to a halt, did an illegal U-turn in the middle of the main road with utter disregard for the Saturday morning traffic, and finally drew up alongside. It was my old friend Ruth, whom I hadn't seen since she'd met me in Cornwall, many months ago.

So it was quite a little procession which arrived at the Palace Pier just before 11 am on Saturday morning, January 31st. Waiting for me at the pier in the bright winter sunshine were my mother and brother, my cousins, various other friends, plus people who'd just heard about the walk on the news. There was also an assortment of representatives from various newspapers, TV and radio stations, and

Arrival in Brighton

for several minutes it seemed as though whenever I turned round yet another microphone was thrust in my face.

How did I feel, they wanted to know. How far had I actually walked? Did my feet hurt? How much weight had I lost?

I think I annoyed everyone by telling the absolute truth, even though it wasn't what they expected and didn't make a particularly good story. For actually the truth was very mundane—I felt fine, but not particularly ecstatic or outrageously happy; my feet didn't hurt at all, and I'd put on weight, not lost it. I didn't manage any memorable quotes or really give them that much to write about or broadcast. And I didn't paddle in the sea. It was no good; I just didn't live up to everyone's image of a long distance walker; in spite of everything I was far too ordinary.

Soon we all made our way to the hotel, which had indeed put on a magnificent spread. My friends and relatives got to drink champagne and enjoy the food, while I just got to answer yet more questions and be photographed over and over again. Such is the lot of a celebrity, I realised. But I had to admit I was rather enjoying all the attention.

So finally the celebration—and the walk—came to an end. Miriam and I took the train back to Croydon, and I settled down to a so-called normal life. I hung up my boots and took out my typewriter, for I had told so many people I planned to write a book about the walk that I decided I'd better actually do it. I found a place to live, got myself a job, and faded quietly back into obscurity. The walk quickly became yesterday's news; I wasn't a celebrity for long.

Actually I discovered that one had to work hard if one wanted to be really famous. Two days after the walk I was asked to travel to Southampton to be interviewed on the TV. I refused, for I'd just moved house and I was surrounded by what seemed like thousands of boxes. Two minutes after this John Lees was on the phone to me.

"You've got to go!" He sounded furious. "How do you expect to get publicity if you turn down the offer of interviews. Do you want to be a secretary for ever? This is your big chance!"

It didn't feel that way to me. I didn't want any more publicity; I was tired of the constant questions and conversations about the walk. It had been good, but it was over. I didn't have plans to do any more; I had no intention of turning into a kind of professional long distance walker; there are more important things to do with one's life. It had been a tremendous adventure, something I would never forget, and I was very glad I had done it. I had learned a lot, both about myself and about Britain and its people. I had found out much about my own capabilities and limitations, and discovered that most things are possible if one really want to do them. Indeed, it had been a valuable and worthwhile experience. And most of all, it had been fun.

Appendix
Routes and Mileages

Day	Date	Route	Distance	Total
1	4/3/86	Brighton—Shoreham—Lancing	9½	9½
2	2/3/86	Lancing—Worthing—Littlehampton—Middleton-on-Sea—Bognor Regis	20	29½
3	3/3/86	Bognor Regis—Pagham—Pagham Harbour—Selsey Bill—Bracklesham Bay—East Wittering	17½	47
4	4/3/86	East Wittering—West Portsmouth Itchenor—Bosham—Southbourne—	21	68
5	5/3/86	Portsmouth—Southsea—Gosport—Lee-on-Solent	17½	85½
6	6/3/86	Lee-on-Solent —Warsash—Hamble—Southampton—Hythe	20	105½
7	7/3/86	Hythe—Beaulieu—Bucklers Hard—Lymington	20½	126
8	8/3/86	Lymington—Milford-on-Sea—Barton-on-Sea—Highcliffe	14½	140½
9	9/3/86	Highcliffe—Southbourne—Boscombe—Bournemouth	13	153½
10	10/3/86	Bournemouth—Sandbanks—Studland—Swanage	16½	170
11	11/3/86	Rest Day	–	170
12	12/3/86	Swanage—Dorset Coast Path—Kimmeridge	15½	185½
13	13/3/86	Kimmeridge—round edge of army range—East Lulworth—West Lulworth	20	205½
14	14/3/86	West Lulworth—Durdle Door—Osmington Mills—Weymouth	18	223½
15	15/3/86	Weymouth—East Fleet—Abbotsbury—Burton Bradstock	21½	245
16	16/3/86	Burton Bradstock—Seatown—Golden Cap—Charmouth—Lyme Regis	15½	260½
17	17/3/86	Lyme Regis—The Landslip—Seaton—Beer—Weston—Sidmouth	22	282½

18	18/3/86	Sidmouth—Budleigh Salterton—Exmouth	18½	301
19	19/3/86	Rest Day	–	301
20	20/3/86	Exmouth—Topsham Ferry—Dawlish	17	318
21	21/3/86	Dawlish—Teignmouth—Shaldon—Torquay	19	337
22	22/3/86	Torquay—Paignton—Brixham—St Mary's Bay	14½	351½
23	23/3/86	St Mary's Bay—Kingswear—Dartmouth—Stoke Fleming	13½	365
24	24/3/86	Stoke Fleming—Torcross—Beesands—Hallsands—East Prawle	12	377
25	25/3/86	East Prawle—Prawle Point—East Portlemouth—Salcombe	8	385
26	26/3/86	Salcombe—Hope Cove—Bantham—Bigbury-on-Sea	11	396
27	27/3/87	Bigbury-on-Sea—River Erme—Moss Mayo—Wembury	18	414
28	28/3/86	Wembury—Plymouth	14	428
29	29/3/86	Rest Day	–	428
30	30/3/86	Plymouth—Cremyll—Cawsand—Rame Head—Portwrinkle	17	445
31	31/3/86	Portwrinkle—Seaton—Millandreath	9	454
32	1/4/86	Millandreath—Looe—Polperro—Polruan	17	471
33	2/4/86	Polruan—Fowey—Par—Charlestown—Higher Porthpean	14	485
34	3/4/86	Higher Porthpean—Mevagissey—Dodman Point—Boswinger	16	501
35	4/4/86	Boswinger—Portloe—Mare Head—Portscatho	16½	517½
36	5/4/86	Portscatho—Percuil—St Mawes—Falmouth	8	525½
37	6/4/86	Falmouth—Helford Passage—Helford—Coverack	19	544½
38	7/4/86	Coverack—Cadgwith—Lizard Point	15	559½
39	8/4/86	Lizard Point—Mullion Cove—Porthleven—Praa Sands	22	581½
40	9/4/86	Praa Sands—Marazion—Penzance	15½	597
41	10/4/86	Rest Day	–	597

42	11/4/86	Penzance—Mousehole—Lamorna—Porthcurno	15	612
43	12/4/86	Porthcurno—Lands End—St Just	12	624
44	13/4/86	St Just—Zennor	14½	638½
45	14/4/86	Zennor—St Ives—Hayle	14½	653
46	15/4/86	Hayle—Portreath—Porthtowan—St Agnes	22½	675½
47	16/4/86	St Agnes—Perranporth—Newquay—Porth Sands	18	693½
48	17/4/86	Porth Sands—Porthcothan—Tryarnon Bay	12	705½
49	18/4/86	Tryarnon Bay—Padstow—Pentire Point—Portquin	21	726½
50	19/4/86	Portquin—Port Isaac—Trebarwith Strand—Tintagel	14	740½
51	20/4/86	Tintagel—Boscastle	9	749½
52	21/4/86	Boscastle—Crackington Haven—Widemouth Bay	11	760½
53	22/4/86	Widemouth Bay—Bude—Elmscott	18	778½
54	23/4/86	Rest Day	–	778½
55	24/4/86	Elmscott—Hartland Quay—Clovelly	16½	795
56	25/4/86	Clovelly—Westward Ho!	15½	810½
57	26/4/86	Westward Ho!—Appledore—Bideford—Barnstaple—Braunton	28½	839
58	27/4/86	Braunton—Croyde Bay—Woolacombe—Ilfracombe	18½	857½
59	28/4/86	Ilfracombe—Combe Martin—Hunters Inn—Lynton	18½	876
60	29/4/86	Lynton—Lynmouth—Porlock Weir—Porlock	16½	892½
61	30/4/86	Porlock—Minehead	10½	903
62	1/5/86	Rest Day	–	903
63	2/5/86	Minehead—Dunster—Watchet—East Quantoxhead—Stolford	27	930
64	3/5/86	Stolford—Combwich—Burnham-on-Sea—Brean	16½	964
65	4/5/86	Brean—Weston-super-Mare—Clevedon	17½	964
66	5/5/86	Clevedon—Avonmouth—Severn Sands Severn Bridge—Chepstow	26	990
67	6/5/76	Rest Day	–	990

68	7/5/86	Chepstow—Caldicot—Newport	19½	1,009½
69	8/5/86	Newport—Cardiff	17	1,026½
70	9/5/86	Cardiff—Penarth—Barry—St Athan	24	1,050½
71	10/5/86	Rest Day	–	1,050½
72	11/5/86	St Athan—Llanwit Major—St Brides Major—Merthyr Mawl—Porthcawl	23½	1,074
73	12/5/86	Porthcawl—Port Talbot—Swansea	22	1,096
74	13/5/86	Swansea—Mumbles—Oxwich—Port Eynon	21	1,117
75	14/5/86	Port Eynon—Rhossili—Llangennith—Crofty	16	1,133
76	15/5/86	Crofty—Llanelli—Trimsaran	15½	1,148½
77	16/5/86	Trimsaran—Kidwelly—Ferryside—Carmarthen—Travellers Rest	23	1,171½
78	17/5/86	Travellers Rest—St Clears—Laugharne— Pendine	18	1,189½
79	18/5/87	Pendine—Amroth—Saundersfoot—Pentlepoir	9½	1,199
80	19/5/86	Rest Day	–	1,199
81	20/5/86	Pentlepoir—Saundersfoot—Tenby—Manorbier—Freshwater East	25½	1,224½
82	21/5/86	Freshwater East—Bosherton—Castlemartin	14½	1,239
83	22/5/86	Castlemartin—Freshwater West—Angle—Pembroke —Llanstadwell	27	1,266
84	23/5/86	Llanstadwell—Sandyhaven Pill—Dale	20½	1,286½
85	24/5/86	Dale—St Ann's Head—Marloes Sands	14	1,300½
86	25/5/86	Marloes Sands—St Brides—Broad Haven—Newgale	18	1,318½
87	26/5/86	Newgale—Solva—St Justinian—St Davids Youth Hostel	17	1,335½
88	27/5/86	Rest Day	–	1,335½
89	28/5/86	Rest Day (walked 3 miles around headland)	3	1,338½
90	29/5/86	St Davids Youth Hostel—Trevine—Pwll Deri	20	1,358½
91	30/5/86	Pwll Deri—Strumble Head—Fishguard—Newport	24	1,382½
92	31/5/86	Newport—Cemaes Head—Poppit Sands	17	1,399½

93	1/6/86	Poppit Sands—Mwnt—Aberporth—Llangranog	22	1,421½
94	2/6/86	Llangranog—Cwmtudu—New Quay	12	1,433½
95	3/6/86	New Quay—Aberaeron—Llanrhystud—Rhydyfelin	24	1,457½
96	4/6/86	Rhydyfelin—Aberystwyth—Borth	11	1,468½
97	5/6/86	Rest Day	–	1,468½
98	6/6/86	Borth—Aberdovey—Tywyn—Fairbourne—Barmouth	23	1,491½
99	7/6/86	Barmouth—Shell Island—Llanbedr	11½	1,503
100	8/6/86	Llanbedr—Harlech—Portmeirion—Porthmadog—Morfa Bychan	22½	1,525½
101	9/6/86	Morfa Bychan—Criccieth—Pwllheli—Llanbedrog	18	1,543½
102	10/6/86	Llanbedrog—Botwnnog—Sarn—Nefyn	21½	1,565
103	11/6/86	Nefyn—Llanaelhaearn—Caernarfon	21½	1,586½
104	12/6/86	Caernarfon—Bangor	12	1,598½
105	13/6/86	Bangor—Penmaenmawr—Conwy—Deganwy	18	1,616½
106	14/6/86	Rest Day	–	1,616½
107	15/6/86	Rest Day	–	1,616½
108	16/6/86	Deganwy—Great Ormes Head—Llandudno—Colwyn Bay	15½	1,632
109	17/6/86	Colwyn Bay—Rhyl—Prestatyn	21	1,653
110	18/6/86	Prestatyn—Flint—Connah's Quay	21	1,674
111	19/6/86	Connah's Quay—Neston—West Kirby	20½	1,694½
112	20/6/86	West Kirby—Hoylake—Wallasey	8½	1,703
113	21/6/86	Wallasey—Liverpool	4½	1,707½
114	22/6/86	Liverpool—Crosby—Formby	16½	1,724
115	23/6/86	Formby—Southport—Much Hoole—Hutton—Preston	30	1,754
116	24/6/86	Preston—Freckleton—Lytham—St Annes	19	1,773
117	25/6/86	St Annes—Blackpool—Fleetwood	17½	1,790½
118	26/6/86	Fleetwood—Knott End—Lancaster	21	1,810½
119	27/6/86	Lancaster—Carnforth—Silverdale—Arnside	23	1,833½
120	28/6/86	Arnside—Silverdale—Across Morecambe Bay—Kents Bank	8	1,841½

121	29/6/86	Kents Bank—Flukeburgh—Ulverston	18	1,859½
122	30/6/86	Ulverston—Goadsbarrow—Barrow-in-Furness—Askam—Ireleth	23	1,882½
123	1/7/86	Ireleth—Kirkby—Foxfield—Millom—Haverigg—Silecroft	21½	1,904
124	2/7/86	Silecroft—Bootle—Ravenglass—Drigg	19	1,923
125	3/7/86	Drigg—Seascale—Sellafield—St Bees	16½	1,939½
126	4/7/86	St Bees—St Bees Head—Whitehaven—Workington	21½	1,961
127	5/7/86	Workington—Maryport—Allonby—Beckfoot	20	1,981
128	6/7/86	Beckfoot—Abbeytown—Newton Arlosh—Bowness-on-Solway—Port Carlisle	20½	2,001½
129	7/7/86	Port Carlisle—Burgh by Sands—Carlisle	14½	2,016
130	8/7/86	Rest Day	–	2,016
131	9/7/86	Carlisle—Gretna—Eastriggs	17	2,033
132	10/7/86	Eastriggs—Annan—Ruthwell—Glencaple	24½	2,057½
133	11/7/86	Glencaple—Dumfries—New Abbey—Southerness	21	2,078½
134	12/7/86	Southerness—Sandyhills Bay—Rockcliffe—Kippford—Palnackie	15½	2,094
135	13/7/86	Palnackie—Auchencairn—Dundrennan—Kirkcudbright—Seaward	22	2,116
136	14/7/86	Seaward—Borgue—Carrick—Gatehouse of Fleet—Carsluith	21½	2,137½
137	15/7/86	Carsluith—Creetown—Newton Stewart—Minnigaff	10	2,147½
138	16/7/86	Rest Day	–	2,147½
139	17/7/86	Minnigaff—Newton Stewart—Wigtown—Garlieston	17½	2,165
140	18/7/86	Garlieston—Isle of Whithorn—Monreith—Port William	19	2,184
141	19/7/86	Port William—Glenluce—Dunragit	20	2,204
142	20/7/86	Dunragit—Stranraer—Cairnryan	13	2,217
143	21/7/86	Cairnryan—Ballantrae—Lendalfoot	19½	2,236½
144	22/7/86	Lendalfoot—Girvan—Turnberry—Maidens—Calzean Country Park	23½	2,260

145	23/7/86	Calzean Country Park—Ayr	14	2,274
146	24/7/86	Rest Day	–	2,274
147	25/7/86	Ayr—Prestwick—Troon—Irvine—Saltcoats—Ardrossan—Brodick	22	2,296
148	26/7/86	Brodick—Corrie—Sannox—Fallen Rocks—Laggan—Cock of Arran—Lochranza	19	2,315
149	27/7/86	Lochranza—Claonaig—Grogport—Carradale	17½	2,332½
150	28/7/86	Carradale—Saddell—Campbeltown	17½	2,350
151	29/7/86	Campbeltown—Bellochantuy—Glenbarr—Muasdale	18	2,368
152	30/7/86	Muasdale—Tayinloan—Clachan—Whitehouse	17½	2,385½
153	31/7/86	Whitehouse—West Tarbert—Kilberry	21½	2,407
154	1/8/86	Kilberry—Achahoish—Ellary—Kilmory—Castle Sween	26	2,433
155	2/8/86	Castle Sween—Achnamara—Bellanoch—Kilmartin	19	2,452
156	3/8/86	Kilmartin—Kilmelford—Kilninver	20	2,472
157	4/8/86	Kilninver—Kilmore—Oban	13	2,485
158	5/8/86	Oban—Craignure	4½	2,489½
159	6/8/86	Craignure—Salen—Tobermory	21	2,510½
160	7/8/86	Rest Day	–	2,510½
161	8/8/86	Tobermory—Mingary—Kilchoan—Point of Ardnamurchan—Sanna - Fascadale	22	2,532½
162	9/8/86	Fascadale—Kilmory—Ockle—Acharacle—Mingarry—Langal	21	2,554
163	10/8/86	Langal—Glenuig—Lochailot—Glen Mama Farm	22	2,576
164	11/8/86	Glen Mama Farm—Arisaig—Back of Keppoch—Garramor	14	2,590
165	12/8/86	Rest Day	–	2,590
166	13/8/86	Garramor—Mallaig—Armadale—Isle Ornsay	17	2,607
167	14/8/86	Isle Ornsay—Breakish—Kyleakin—Kyle of Lochalsh—Plockton	25	2,632
168	15/8/86	Plockton—Stromeferry—Strathcarron—Lochcarron	19	2,651

169	16/8/86	Lochcarron—Kishorn—Pass of the Cattle—Applecross	20	2,671
170	17/8/86	Applecross—Cuaig—Fearnmore—Kenmore	17½	2,688½
171	18/8/86	Kenmore—Sheildaig—Torridon	17	2,705½
172	19/8/86	Rest Day	–	2,705½
173	20/8/86	Torridon—Inveralligan—Lower Daibaig—Craig Youth Hostel	14	2,719½
174	21/8/86	Craig Youth Hostel—Redpoint—Badachro	13	2,732½
175	22/8/86	Rest Day	–	2,732½
176	23/8/86	Badachro—Gairloch—Poolewe—Aultbea—Laide	22½	2,755
177	24/8/86	Laide—Badcaul—Dundonnel	18	2,773
178	25/8/86	Dundonnel—Altnaharrie—Ullapool	8	2,781
179	26/8/86	Rest Day	–	2,781
180	27/8/86	Ullapool—Rock Path—Achininver	16	2,797
181	28/8/86	Achininver—Achiltibuie—Inverkirkaig	22	2,819
182	29/8/86	Inverkirkaig—Lochinver—Achmelvich	10	2,829
183	30/8/86	Achmelvich—Stoer—Drumbeg—Glenleraig	14½	2,843½
184	31/8/86	Glenleraig—Kylesku—Scourie	20	2,863½
185	1/9/86	Scourie—Laxford Bridge—Rhiconich—Kinlochbervie	18½	2,882
186	2/9/86	Kinlochbervie—Sandwood Bay—Cape Wrath	21	2,903
187	3/9/86	Cape Wrath—Kyle of Durness—Durness	17	2,920
188	4/9/86	Rest Day	–	2,920
189	5/9/86	Durness—Laid—Hope—Tongue	28	2,948
190	6/9/86	Rest Day	–	2,948
191	7/9/86	Tongue—Skerray—Bettyhill	15	2,963
192	8/9/86	Bettyhill—Melvich—Reay	23	2,986
193	9/9/86	Reay—Dounreay—Thurso	17	3,003
194	10/9/86	Thurso—Castletown—Dunnet—Dunnet Head—Brough—West Dunnet	23½	3,026½
195	11/9/86	West Dunnet—Brough—Scarfskerry—East Canisbay	14½	3,041
196	12/9/86	Rest Day	–	3,041

197	13/9/86	East Canisbay—John o'Groats—Duncansby Head—Freswick—Keiss	19	3,060
198	14/9/86	Keiss—Wick—Corbiego—Thrumster	21	3,081
199	15/9/86	Thrumster—Mains of Ulbster—Lybster—Latheron—Dunbeath	21	3,102
200	16/9/86	Dunbeath—Berriedale—Helmsdale	18	3,120
201	17/9/86	Helmsdale—Brora—Golspie	21	3,141
202	18/9/86	Golspie—The Mound—Embo—Dornoch—Clashmore	20	3,161
203	19/9/86	Clashmore—Bonar Bridge—Ardgay	12	3,173
204	20/9/86	Rest Day	–	3,173
205	21/9/86	Ardgay—Edderton—Tain	17	3,190
206	22/9/86	Tain—Arabella—Migg Ferry—Cromarty	13½	3,203½
207	23/9/86	Cromarty—Rosemarkie—Fortrose—Avoch—Corrachie	20	3,223½
208	24/9/86	Corrachie—Munlochy—North Kessock—Inverness	11	3,234½
209	25/9/86	Rest Day	–	3,234½
210	26/9/86	Rest Day	–	3,234½
211	27/9/86	Inverness—Fort George—Nairn	24½	3,259
212	28/9/86	Nairn—Forres—Findhorn	20	3,279
213	29/9/86	Findhorn—Burghead—Hopeman—Duffus	16½	3,295½
214	30/9/86	Duffus—Gordonstoun—Lossiemouth—Kingston—Spey Bay	19½	3,315
215	1/10/86	Spey Bay—Port Gordon—Buckie—Findochty—Portknockie	13	3,328
216	2/10/86	Portknockie—Cullen—Portsoy—Banff—Macduff	25	3,353
217	3/10/86	Macduff—Pennan—Rosehearty—Fraserburgh	25½	3,378½
218	4/10/86	Fraserburgh—Inverallochy—St Combs—Rattray Head—Peterhead	21	3,399½
219	5/10/86	Peterhead—Cruden Bay—Newburgh	27½	3,427
220	6/10/86	Newburgh—Aberdeen	18	3,445
221	7/10/86	Rest Day	–	3,445
222	8/10/86	Aberdeen—Cove Bay—Portlethen—Stonehaven	23	3,468

223	9/10/86	Stonehaven—Inverbervie—Johnshaven—St Cyrus	20	3,488
224	10/10/86	St Cyrus—Montrose—Lunan Bay—Auchmithie	19	3,507
225	11/10/86	Auchmithie—Arbroath—Carnoustie—Monifieth	18½	3,525½
226	12/10/86	Monifieth—Broughton Ferry—Dundee—Newport-on-Tay—Wormit	11½	3,537
227	13/10/86	Rest Day	–	3,537
228	14/10/86	Wormit—Newport-on-Tay—Tayport—Leuchars—St Andrews	17	3,554
229	15/10/86	Rest Day	–	3,554
230	16/10/86	St Andrews—Crail—Anstruther	19	3,573
231	17/10/86	Anstruther—St Monance—Elie—Largo—Leven	20½	3,593½
232	18/10/86	Leven—Methil—Wemyss—Kirkcaldy—Kinghorn	18	3,611½
233	19/10/86	Kinghorn—Burnt Island—Aberdour—Forth Road Bridge—Queensferry	16	3,627½
234	20/10/86	Rest Day	–	3,627½
235	21/10/86	Queensferry—Cramond—Leith	17	3,644½
236	22/10/86	Rest Day	–	3,644½
237	23/10/86	Rest Day	–	3,644½
238	24/10/86	Rest Day	–	3,644½
239	25/10/86	Leith—Portobello—Musselburgh—Longniddry—Aberlady	22½	3,667
240	26/10/86	Aberlady—Gullane—North Berwick—Seacliff	16½	3,683½
241	27/10/86	Seacliff—Tyninghame—Dunbar	16	3,699½
242	28/10/86	Dunbar—Cockburnspath	$12^1/_2$	3,712
243	29/10/86	Cockburnspath—Coldingham—St Abbs	19	3,731
244	30/10/86	St Abbs—Eyemouth—Burnmouth—Berwick-on-Tweed	17	3,748
245	31/10/86	Berwick-on-Tweed—Spittal—Holy Island Causeway—Belford	20	3,768
246	1/11/86	Belford—Bamburgh—Seahouses—Beadnell—Rock	23	3,791
247	2/11/86	Rest Day	–	3,791
248	3/11/86	Rock—Craster—Boulmer—Alnmouth	15	3,806

249	4/11/86	Alnmouth—Warkworth—Amble—South Broomhill	13½	3,819½
250	5/11/86	South Broomhill—Cresswell—Lynemouth—Newbiggin—Blyth	19	3,838
251	6/11/86	Blyth—Whitley Bay—North Shields—South Shields—Whitburn	18	3,856
252	7/11/86	Rest Day	–	3,856
253	8/11/86	Whitburn—Sunderland—Seaham—Peterlee	21	3,877½
254	9/11/86	Peterlee—Horden—Hartlepool—Seaton Carew	15	3,892½
255	10/11/86	Seaton Carew—Middlesborough—Redcar	21	3,913½
256	11/11/86	Redcar—Saltburn—Skinningrove—Boulby—Staithes	19½	3,933
257	12/11/86	Staithes—Runswick Bay—Sandsend—Whitby	17	3,950
258	13/11/86	Rest Day	–	3,950
259	14/11/86	Whitby—Robin Hood's Bay—Boggle Hole Youth Hostel	13	3,963
260	15/11/86	Boggle Hole Youth Hostel—Scarborough	16½	3,979½
261	16/11/86	Scarborough—Cayton Bay—Filey	17½	3,997
262	17/11/86	Filey—Reighton—Bempton—Flamborough—Bridlington	21½	4,018½
263	18/11/86	Bridlington—Skipsea—Atwick—Hornsea	17½	4,036
264	19/11/86	Hornsea—Aldbrough—Withernsea	23	4,059
265	20/11/86	Withernsea—Kilnsea—Skeffling—Patrington	23½	4,082½
266	21/11/86	Patrington—Hedon—Hull	20½	4,103
267	22/11/86	Rest Day	–	4,103
268	23/11/86	Rest Day	–	4,103
269	24/11/86	Hull—Hessle—Humber Bridge—Barton-upon-Humber	11½	4,114½
270	25/11/86	Barton-upon-Humber—New Holland—Immingham	21½	4,136
271	26/11/86	Immingham—Grimsby—Cleethorpes	12	4,148
272	27/11/86	Cleethorpes—North Cotes—North Somercotes	16	4,164

273	28/11/86	North Somercotes—Saltfleet—Maplethorpe—Sutton-on-Sea	16½	4,180½
274	29/11/86	Rest Day	–	4,180½
275	30/11/86	Sutton-on-Sea—Chapel St Leonard's—Ingoldmells—Skegness	16	4,196½
276	1/12/86	Skegness—Gibraltar Point—Friskney	15½	4,212
277	2/12/86	Friskney—Wrangle—Boston	18	4,230
278	3/12/86	Rest Day	–	4,230
279	4/12/86	Boston—Frampton—Fosdyke Bridge—Saracens Head—Fleet Hargate	20	4,250½
280	5/12/86	Fleet Hargate—Long Sutton—Sutton Bridge—Terrington St Clement—West Lynn—Kings Lynn	20½	4,271
281	6/12/86	Kings Lynn—North Wootton	6	4,277
282	7/12/86	Rest Day	–	4,277
283	8/12/86	North Wootton—Castle Rising—Wolferton—Hunstanton	19½	4,296½
284	9/12/86	Rest Day	–	4,296½
285	10/12/86	Rest Day	–	4,296½
286	11/12/86	Hunstanton—Thornham—Brancaster—Burnham Market—Burnham Overy Town	19	4,315½
287	12/12/86	Burnham Overy Town—Holkham—Wells next the Sea—Morston—Blakeney	15½	4,331
288	13/12/86	Blakeney—Cley next the Sea—Saltmarsh—Weybourne—Sheringham	13	4,344
289	14/12/86	Sheringham—Cromer—Mundesley—Bacton	16½	4,360½
290	15/12/86	Bacton—Happisburgh—Horsey—Martham	20	4,380½
291	16/12/86	Martham—Winterton-on-Sea—Caister—Great Yarmouth	13½	4,394
292	17/12/86	Rest Day	–	4,394
293	18/12/86	Great Yarmouth—Gorleston—Corton—Lowestoft	17½	4,411½
294	19/12/86	Rest Day	–	4,411½
295	20/12/86	Lowestoft—Kessingland—Southwold	16	4,427½
296	21/12/86	Southwold—Dunwich—Leiston—Saxmundham	20	4,447½

297	22/12/86	Saxmundham—Snape—Blaxhall	9	4,456½
298	23/12/86	Rest Day	–	4,456½
299	24/12/86	Rest Day	–	4,456½
300	25/12/86	Rest Day	–	4,456½
301	26/12/86	Rest Day	–	4,456½
302	27/12/86	Blaxhall—Woodbridge	13	4,469½
303	28/12/86	Woodbridge—Waldringfield— Felixstoweferry—Felixstowe	17½	4,487
304	29/12/86	Felixstowe—Harwich—Great Oakley— Walton-on-the-Naze	21	4,508
305	30/12/86	Walton-on-the-Naze—Frinton-on-Sea— Clacton-on-Sea	10	4,518
306	31/12/86	Clacton-on-Sea—St Osyth—Thor- rington—Colchester	21	4,539
307	1/1/87	Colchester—Abberton—Peldon—Tol- leshunt Knights	17	4,556
308	2/1/87	Rest Day	–	4,556
309	3/1/87	Tolleshunt Knights—Goldhanger— Maldon	18	4,574
310	4/1/87	Maldon—Latchingdon—Steeple— Bradwell-on-Sea—Tillingham	17½	4,591½
311	5/1/87	Tillingham—Burnham-on-Crouch— Wallasea Island	17	4,608½
312	6/1/87	Wallasea Island—Rochford—Thorpe Bay—Southend—Leigh-on- Sea	21	4,629½
313	7/1/87	Rest Day	–	4,629½
314	8/1/87	Leigh-on-Sea—Pitsea—Vange—Stan- ford- le-Hope	15½	4,645
315	9/1/87	Stanford-le-Hope—East Tilbury—Til- bury—Gravesend	16½	4,661½
316	10/1/87	Gravesend—Cooling—High Halstow—Chattenden—Rochester	22½	4,68½
317	11/1/87	Rochester—Gillingham—Sittingbourne	18	4,702
318	12/1/87	Sittingbourne—Teynham—Faversham	14½	4,716½
319	13/1/87	Faversham—Whitstable	11½	4,728
320	4/1/87	Whitstable—Herne Bay	12	4,740
321	15/1/87	Herne Bay—Birchington—Westgate— Margate	14½	4,754½
322	16/1/87	Margate—Broadstairs—Ramsgate	12	4,766½
323	17/1/87	Rest Day	–	4,766½

324	18/1/87	Ramsgate—Sandwich—Deal	16	4,782½
325	19/1/87	Deal—St Margaret's at Cliffe—Dover	16	4,798½
326	20/1/87	Dover—Folkestone—Sandgate—Hythe—Palmarsh	17½	4,816
327	21/1/87	Rest Day	–	4,816
328	22/1/87	Palmarsh—Dymchurch—Greatstone—Lydd-on-Sea—Lydd	19	4,835½
329	23/1/87	Lydd—Camber—Rye—Winchelsea—Icklesham	19	4,854½
330	24/1/87	Rest Day	–	4,854½
331	25/1/87	Icklesham—Hastings—Bexhill	16½	4,871
332	26/1/87	Bexhill—Pevensey Bay—Eastbourne—Beachy Head Youth Hostel	19	4,890
333	27/1/87	Beachy Head Youth Hostel—Beachy Head—Birling Gap—Seven Sisters—Seaford	15	4,905
334	28/1/87	Rest Day	–	4,905
335	29/1/87	Rest Day	–	4,905
336	30/1/87	Seaford—Newhaven—Saltdean—Rottingdean	12	4,917
337	31/1/87	Rottingdean—Brighton	5	4,922

An Update – March 2007

So what happened next? This is the question that everyone tends to ask after reading a personal account like mine. Did I really "fade quietly into obscurity"? Did my life become perfectly average and normal, from then on?

For a while this was indeed the case. I settled down in Croydon, went back to doing part time secretarial work, and wrote this book. Originally Gollancz were supposed to be publishing it, but then they changed their minds; the publishing industry was struggling at the time, and they weren't sure if my book would make them any money. Then I found another publisher—a small one—but they went out of business at the last minute. So I shelved all publication plans for a while, because by then I was involved in moving to North Wales. I wanted to live in a rural area, and I liked Wales. An added plus was that Miriam was about to move there, which meant that I would know someone in the vicinity.

I lived quietly in Wales for several years. I had found a lovely old cottage on a hillside near Llangollen, with a beautiful view, where I lived with varying numbers of cats for company. I earned my living doing freelance research and writing, and I learned to speak the Welsh language quite fluently. I did no more long walks—or no longer than day rambles near my new home or in Snowdonia. Just like normal people, in fact!

After a few years I decided to self-publish *Midges, Maps & Muesli*. I knew many people who wanted copies, and they persuaded me that my book should see the light of day. The book was well received, and there was some local publicity soon after it first came out. But this soon died down, and I just continued to live a quiet, contented life in my rural backwater.

Then in the late 1990s this all changed. Firstly, in November 1996 my mother died. Two weeks later my favourite cat died, followed a very short time after that by my Buddhist teacher. This all hit me very hard. I felt as though everyone whom I loved and who loved me had gone. On top of that I fell out with my brother, now my only close relative. I became depressed and run down, then caught a bad dose of flu, which left me feeling even more miserable. Soon afterwards, back at work but not yet completely recovered, I happened to pass Welshpool Airfield on my return from a meeting for a research report I was writing. On impulse I booked a trial lesson in a light aircraft, more as a way of trying to cheer myself up than anything else. But I loved it! And as I knew that I was about to inherit quite a lot of money

once my mother's affairs were sorted out, I decided to learn to fly.

I wasn't a natural pilot by any means, and 49 is not a particularly good age to learn something new. The minimum number of hours for a Private Pilot's Licence (PPL) is 45; the national average about 60 ... it took me 80. But once I got that licence, this hardly mattered. I paired up with another new pilot, and that first summer, we flew and flew. We went to many new places, got lost on the way back from Oxford, were stranded overnight in Blackpool due to thunderstorms. Our aerial adventures culminated in a flight to Cornwall in August 1999 to watch the total eclipse, and unlike many on that cloudy day, we saw it.

So what could I do next? I was now totally addicted to new aerial adventures and experiences, and I wanted more. So I decided to have a trial helicopter lesson. It was just to experience something different, and I told my friends that helicopter flying was too expensive, and that even if I liked it I wouldn't take it up. They never let me forget that comment! For I managed to hover the machine by myself on that first lesson, and that got me hooked. Helicopter flying was amazing;

these little machines were so versatile, they could go anywhere, do almost anything. I went back for more, and soon realised that I might as well stop fooling myself—I was going to get a PPL(H) or Private Pilot's Helicopter Licence. After all, I had the money, my inheritance having come through by now. So why not?

I enjoyed my PPL(H) course, which I did over the next year. But towards the end of it I began to get a little worried. An inheritance is not a regenerating money tree, and I knew that I couldn't afford to keep flying helicopters regularly for ever. But by now I was familiar with the aviation world, and I was aware that many people got commercial helicopter licences in their 30s and 40s, since they often couldn't afford it till then. So I began to wonder ...

My decision was made the day of my final flight test.

"You've passed," said the examiner.

"Well, can you tell me about getting a commercial licence," I replied.

Without turning a hair he said: "Well, shall we do the paperwork for this one first?"

We did, and then he told me what I'd now have to do—14 exams of around degree level, in a range of subjects such as navigation, meteorology, principles of rotary flight, radio aids, aircraft engines and electrics, etc; followed by a 30-hour Commercial Flying Course. Could I do it? I really didn't know. I hadn't passed any exams for years, and I'd never been very technically minded in the first place. But I decided to give it a go.

I spent the following winter studying for the exams, then booked myself on a short crammer course, hoping they'd explain some of the things which I was struggling with. I found it all quite hard, and had to re-sit a couple of exams, but by the summer I had passed the lot. So that autumn I did the flying course, again finding it difficult but managing to pass.

I was now in an awkward position. A Commercial Helicopter Licence and around 200 flying hours is a bit like a degree in some obscure subject—it sounds impressive, but no-one will employ you without more experience. I wanted to instruct anyway; I liked working with people as much as I liked helicopter flying, so this had been my goal from the start. But I needed another 100 flying hours before I could do the Flying Instructor Course, and I realised that I would probably have to pay for them. Flying is much cheaper overseas, so I decided to combine getting these hours with two holidays, albeit rather busy ones. So that spring I went to Southern California for three weeks, and then in the summer I spent ten days in Russia, experiencing things like mountain flying, and flying ex-military Russian helicopters—things which I could never have done in the UK.

By January 2003 I had all the flying experience I needed, and I started my Instructors' Course. This turned out to be the toughest thing I'd ever done. I hated it, was ready to give up, and became convinced I'd never be able to fly well enough to pass. Then I became ill, and abandoned the whole thing just before the final test. But after I recovered and had a short break, and with a little help and encouragement from friends and old instructors, I managed to pass. I was a helicopter instructor at last!

I had never intended to instruct fulltime; I had a well paid research and writing job, and flying is insecure and weather dependent. So for three years I instructed at weekends, gradually gaining more experience and confidence. I also began writing now and then for the aviation magazines. I gradually began to get better known for this aviation writing, and in 2004 I was nominated for one of the Aerospace Journalist of the Year Awards—the Oscars of the aviation writing world. I didn't win, but the nomination and subsequent publicity got me more writing work, and I soon began to write regularly for a couple of publications. So by 2005 I was commuting to Tatenhill Airfield, near Burton-on-Trent in Staffordshire, and instructing there two days a week, and I was also travelling all over the country for my aviation writing. I was seeing less and less of my home in Wales, and becoming more and more familiar—far too familiar—with the M54 and A5, the roads which took me from North Wales to the Midlands. It wasn't making any sense to carry on living where I was. So I began to consider moving again, to somewhere more accessible.

I might well have gone on thinking about the proposed move for years, since I loved my cottage on the hillside. But later that year some of my longer term research and writing work, on which I had relied for an income, began to dry up. That decided me once and for all—it was time to leave Wales. I began to look in earnest for a house in Derbyshire, around the southern end of the Peak District, an area I knew quite well and had always liked. It was rural and beautiful, but near the motorway system—and also close to a number of airfields including Tatenhill.

So in early 2006 I moved to a small village near Ashbourne, along with my five cats. I carried on instructing part time at Tatenhill, and the following summer a flying school in Sheffield also gave me some work. So almost by chance I found myself working as a fulltime helicopter instructor. It was hard work, but I loved it. And when the weather was bad, or during quiet winter periods, I continued with my aviation writing, finding that the two careers slotted together extremely well. And as I started getting known as an aviation writer, so this book was suddenly rediscovered by the public. Sales of Midges, Maps & Muesli gradually began to increase—I had a new generation of readers, who knew my current writing, and wanted to know what had come before. Soon I had almost no copies left, and realised that I would have to republish it.

If anyone had told me ten years ago that at the age of 54 I would become a helicopter instructor and aviation writer, I would have thought they were quite mad. I had never even really considered learning to fly, until that day in early 1997 when I stopped at Welshpool Airfield. I had always liked trying new things, it is true, as must be obvious to everyone who knows anything about me. And I had also never really found a career which suited me. But I still can't quite believe that at an age when many of my friends are taking early retirement, I have a new career—flying these wonderful little machines, writing about them, and sometimes fulfilling people's life-long dreams. To understand that last comment, you need to read the following account, which is actually fairly typical of one of my trial lessons on a normal working day:

"I'm doing....what? A helicopter flight!!"

The speaker was an elderly lady, leaning heavily on her stick. It was her 75th birthday, and she'd thought she was going to a car boot sale. Instead, her relatives had bought her a trial helicopter lesson/air experience flight, and I was her instructor. It had come as a complete surprise, and as I led her out to the helicopter, she got a bit panicky. "I'll never be able to climb in," she said.

"Don't worry," I reassured her, "I'll get one of the fire crew to help you".

Once aboard, she was fine; she had always wanted to fly a helicopter, and couldn't wait to have a go on the controls. Half an hour later she was glowing happily, with that ear-to-ear grin which we instructors recognise so well.

"Thank you," she said. "That was the greatest experience of my life".

For me, life doesn't get much better than that.

Lightning Source UK Ltd.
Milton Keynes UK
18 August 2010

158603UK00008B/31/A